SAXON®

Adaptations for Algebra 1, Geometry, Algebra 2

Student Reference Guide

SAXON®

HOUGHTON MIFFLIN HARCOURT
Supplemental Publishers

www.SaxonPublishers.com
800-531-5015

ISBN 13: 978-1-6027-7505-3
ISBN 10: 1-6027-7505-2

Printed in the United States of America

13 1838 21 4500819636

Table of Contents

Algebra 1

Algebra Foundations

Functions and Relations

Equations and Inequalities

Polynomials

Probability and Data Analysis

Geometry

Geometry

Geometry Foundations

Triangles, Congruence, and Similarity

Circles

Polygons

Right Triangles and Trigonometry

Coordinate Geometry

Solids

Logic and Reasoning

Algebra 2

Linear/Quadratic Functions

Polynomials and Polynomial Functions

Rational and Radical Functions

Exponential and Logarithmic Functions

Linear Systems/Matrices

Conic Sections

Trigonometry

Probability and Statistics

Sequences, Series, and Logic

Algebra Foundations

Subsets of Real Numbers	
Natural Numbers	The numbers used to count objects or things. $\{1, 2, 3, 4, \ldots\}$
Whole Numbers	The set of natural numbers and zero. $\{0, 1, 2, 3, 4, \ldots\}$
Integers	The set of whole numbers and the opposites of the natural numbers. $\{\ldots, -4, -3, -2, -1, 0, 1, 2, 3, 4, \ldots\}$
Rational Numbers	Numbers that can be written in the form $\frac{a}{b}$, where a and b are integers and $b \neq 0$. In decimal form, rational numbers either terminate or repeat. Examples: $\frac{1}{2}$, $0.\overline{3}$, $-\frac{2}{3}$, 0.125
Irrational Numbers	Numbers that cannot be written as the quotient of two integers. In decimal form, irrational numbers neither terminate nor repeat. Examples: $\sqrt[3]{5}$, $\sqrt{2}$, $-\sqrt{2}$, $3\sqrt{3}$, π, 3π
Real Numbers	The set including all rational and irrational numbers.

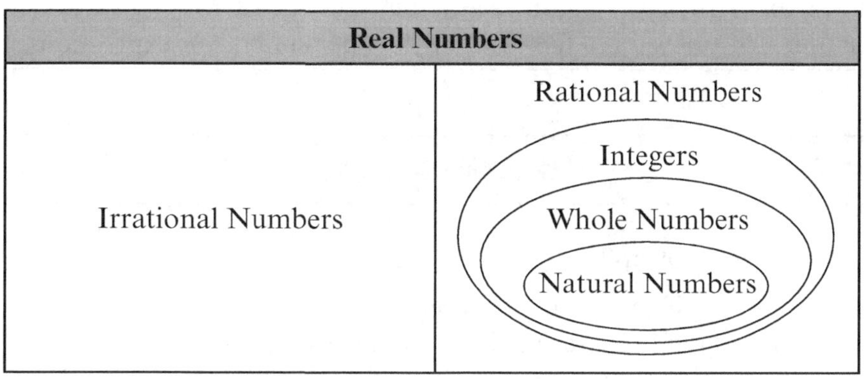

Closed Set for Real Numbers
A set of numbers is closed under a given operation if the outcome of the operation on any two members of the set is also a member of the set.

Intersection/Union of Sets
The **intersection of sets** A and B, $A \cap B$, is the set of elements that are in A and B. The **union** of A and B, $A \cup B$, is the set of all elements that are in A or B.

Algebra Foundations

Order of Operations
1. Work inside grouping symbols.
2. Simplify powers and roots.
3. Multiply and divide from left to right.
4. Add and subtract from left to right.

Percent of Increase/Decrease
Percent of Increase
$\frac{\text{amount of increase}}{\text{original amount}}$
Percent of Decrease
$\frac{\text{amount of decrease}}{\text{original amount}}$

Factors
Factors of 6: 1, 2, 3, 6
Factors of 9: 1, 3, 9
GCF of 6 and 9 $\longrightarrow$ 3
The greatest common factor of an expression is the product of the greatest integer and the greatest power of each variable that divides evenly into each term of the expression.
GCF of $6x^3y$ and $9x^2y^2$ $\longrightarrow$ $3x^2y$

Finding the Least Common Multiple
1. Write each number as a product of prime factors.
2. Use every factor of the given numbers as a factor of the LCM. Use each factor the greatest number of times it is a factor of any of the numbers or expressions.

Tests for Divisibility

A number is able to be divided by . . .

2	if the last digit is even.
4	if the last two digits can be divided by 4.
8	if the last three digits can be divided by 8.
5	if the last digit is 0 or 5.
10	if the last digit is 0.
3	if the **sum of the digits** can be divided by 3.
6	if the number can be divided by 2 **and** by 3.
9	if the **sum of the digits** can be divided by 9.

Algebra Foundations

Properties of Addition and Multiplication	
Identity Property of Addition	
Adding 0.	Example: $5 + 0 = 5$
Identity Property of Multiplication	
Multiplying by 1.	Example: $5 \cdot 1 = 5$
Commutative Property of Addition or Multiplication	
Order is changed.	Example: $5 + 2 = 2 + 5$ $5 \cdot 2 = 2 \cdot 5$
Associative Property of Addition or Multiplication	
Groups are changed.	Example: $(1 + 2) + 3 = 1 + (2 + 3)$ $(1 \cdot 2) \cdot 3 = 1 \cdot (2 \cdot 3)$

The Distributive Property	
$x(y + z)$	Example: $5(2 + 1) = 5 \cdot 2 + 5 \cdot 1 = 15$
$x(y - z)$	Example: $5(2 - 1) = 5 \cdot 2 + 5 \cdot -1 = 5$

Cross Products Property
If $\frac{a}{b} = \frac{c}{d}$ and $b \neq 0$ and $d \neq 0$, then $ad = bc$.
In $\frac{a}{b} \times \frac{c}{d}$, ad and bc are the **cross products.**

Properties of Real Numbers	
Multiplication Property of −1	
Change the sign.	Example: $9 \cdot -1 = -1 \cdot 9 = -9$
Multiplication Property of Zero	
Anything times 0 is 0.	Example: $9 \cdot 0 = 0$
Inverse Property of Multiplication	
A number times its reciprocal is 1.	Example: $3 \cdot \frac{1}{3} = \frac{1}{3} \cdot 3 = 1$

Multiplying and Dividing Signed Numbers		
Same signs: product or quotient is positive.	$(+)(+) = (+)$ $(+) \div (+) = (+)$	$(-)(-) = (+)$ $(-) \div (-) = (+)$
Opposite signs: product or quotient is negative.	$(+)(-) = (-)$ $(+) \div (-) = (-)$	$(-)(+) = (-)$ $(-) \div (+) = (-)$

Algebra Foundations

Product Property of Radicals

If a and b are non-negative real numbers, then

$$\sqrt{a}\sqrt{b} = \sqrt{ab} \quad \text{and} \quad \sqrt{ab} = \sqrt{a}\sqrt{b}.$$

Quotient Property of Radicals

If $m \geq 0$ and $n > 0$, then $\frac{\sqrt{m}}{\sqrt{n}} = \sqrt{\frac{m}{n}}$ and $\sqrt{\frac{m}{n}} = \frac{\sqrt{m}}{\sqrt{n}}$.

Higher-Order Roots

If $a^n = b$, then the nth root of b is a, or $\sqrt[n]{b} = a$. The n to the left of the radical sign in the expression is the index of the radical. The index is an integer greater than or equal to 2.

Fractional Exponents

$$\sqrt[n]{b} = b^{\frac{1}{n}}$$

Product Property of Exponents

If m and n are real numbers and $x \neq 0$, then

$$x^m \cdot x^n = x^{m+n}.$$

Quotient Property of Exponents

If m and n are real numbers and $x \neq 0$, then

$$\frac{x^m}{x^n} = x^{m-n} = \frac{1}{x^{n-m}}$$

$$\frac{5^4}{5^2} = 5^{4-2} = 5^2 = 25 \qquad \frac{5^2}{5^4} = \frac{1}{5^{4-2}} = \frac{1}{5^2} = \frac{1}{25}$$

Negative Exponent

For every nonzero number x, $x^{-n} = \frac{1}{x^n}$ and $x^n = \frac{1}{x^{-n}}$.

Zero Exponent Property

For every nonzero number x, $x^0 = 1$.

Algebra Foundations

Power of a Power Property
If m and n are real numbers and $x \neq 0$, then $$(x^m)^n = x^{mn}.$$

Power of a Product Property
If m is a real number with $x \neq 0$ and $y \neq 0$, then $$(xy)^m = x^m y^m.$$

Power of a Quotient Property
If x and y are any nonzero real numbers and m is an integer, then $$\left(\frac{x}{y}\right)^m = \frac{x^m}{y^m}.$$

Functions and Relations

Definition of a Function
A type of relation that pairs each element in the domain with exactly one element in the range.

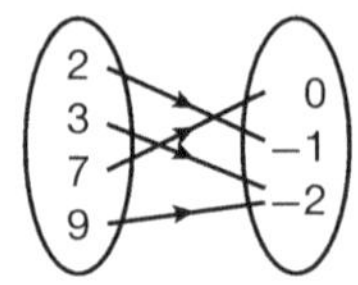

Linear Equations
Slope formula
$m = \frac{y_2 - y_1}{x_2 - x_1}$
Slope-intercept form
$y = mx + b$
Point-slope form
$y - y_1 = m(x - x_1)$
Standard form
$Ax + By = C$

Quadratic Equations
Standard form
$ax^2 + bx + c = 0$
Axis of symmetry
$x = -\frac{b}{2a}$
Quadratic formula
$x = \frac{-b \pm \sqrt{b^2 - 4ac}}{2a}$

Using the Discriminant
For the quadratic equation $ax^2 + bx + c = 0$ where $a \neq 0$, find the value of the discriminant, $b^2 - 4ac$, to determine the number of real solutions, which represents the number of x-intercepts of the graph of its related function. If $b^2 - 4ac < 0$, then there are no real solutions and no x-intercepts. If $b^2 - 4ac = 0$, then there is one real solution and one x-intercept. If $b^2 - 4ac > 0$, then there are two real solutions and two x-intercepts.

Zero Product Property
If the product of two quantities equals zero, at least one of the quantities equals zero.

Direct variation
$y = kx$

Joint Variation
A relationship among three variables that can be written in the form of $y = kxz$, where $k \neq 0$.

Inverse variation
$y = \frac{k}{x}; x \neq 0$

Product Rule for Inverse Variation
If (x_1, y_1) and (x_2, y_2) are solutions of an inverse variation, then $x_1y_1 = x_2y_2$.

Functions and Foundations

The Distance Formula

The distance d between two points (x_1, y_1) and (x_2, y_2) is
$$d = \sqrt{(x_2 - x_1)^2 + (y_2 - y_1)^2}.$$

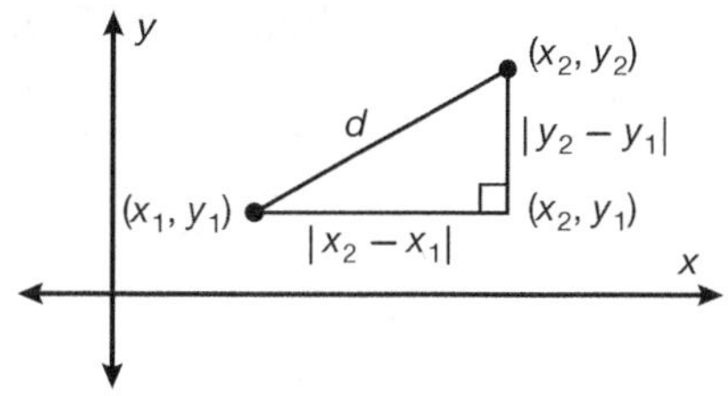

The Midpoint Formula

The midpoint M of the line segment with endpoints (x_1, y_1) and (x_2, y_2) is
$$M = \left(\frac{x_1 + x_2}{2}, \frac{y_1 + y_2}{2}\right).$$

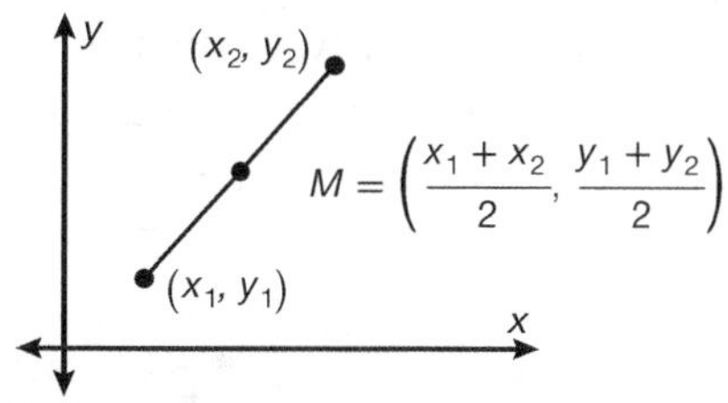

Exponential Decay

$y = kb^x;\ k > 0,\ 0 < b < 1$

Exponential Growth

$y = kb^x;\ k > 0,\ b > 1$

Slopes of Parallel Lines

Two nonvertical lines are parallel if they have the same slope and are not the same line.

Any two vertical lines are parallel.

Example: $y = 2x + 7$ and $y = 2x - 1$

Parallel lines have the same slope and different y-intercepts.

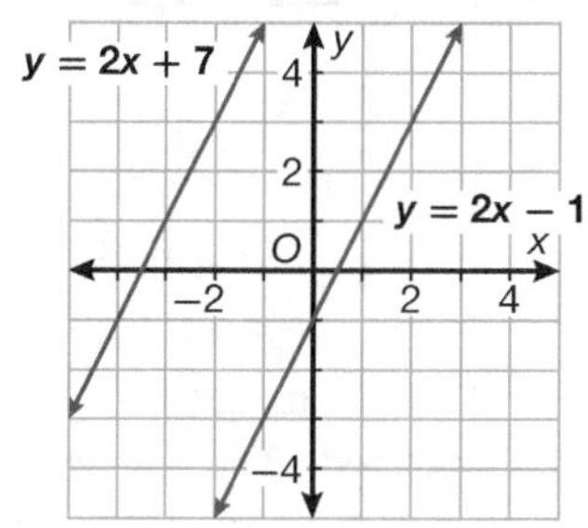

Slopes of Perpendicular Lines

Any two lines are perpendicular if their slopes are negative reciprocals of each other. A vertical and horizontal line are also perpendicular.

Example: $y = 3x - 7$ and $y = \frac{-1}{3}x + 3$

The slopes of perpendicular lines are negative reciprocals.

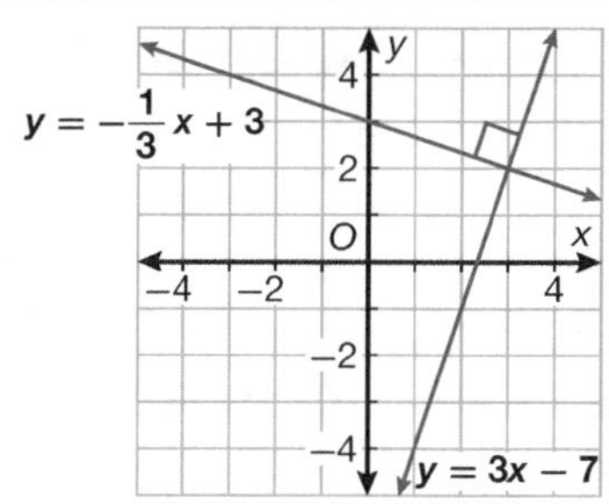

Functions and Relations

Vertical-Line Test	
A graph on the coordinate plane represents a function if any vertical line intersects the graph in exactly one point.	
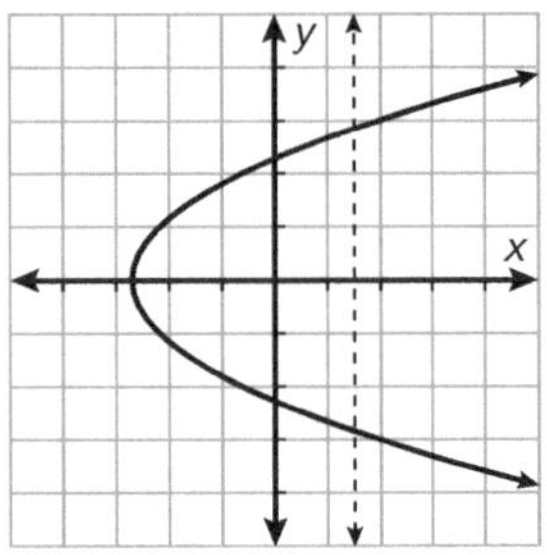	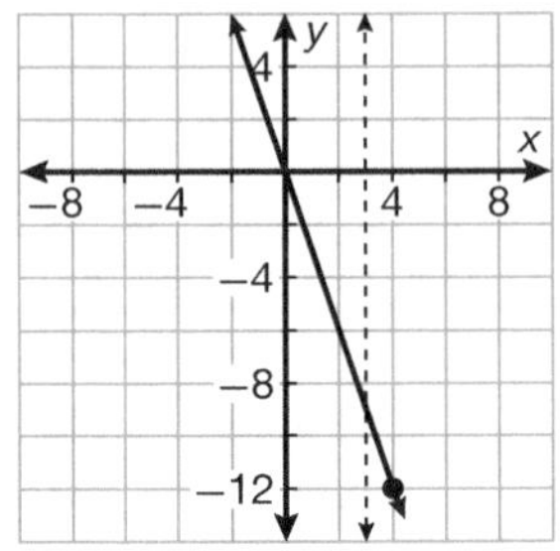
The relation is not a function. The vertical line cuts the graph in more than one place.	The relation is a function. The vertical line cuts the graph in exactly one place.

Systems of Linear Equations		
Consistent and Independent	**Consistent and Dependent**	**Inconsistent**
Exactly One Solution	Infinitely Many Solutions	No Solution
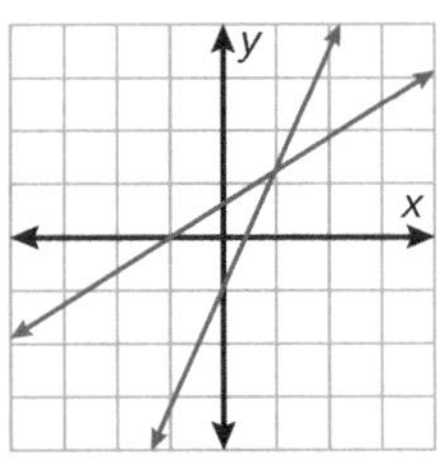	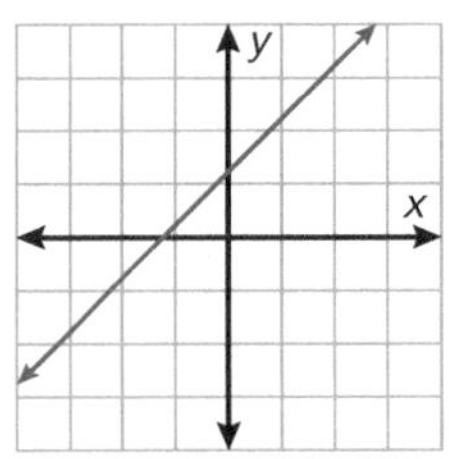	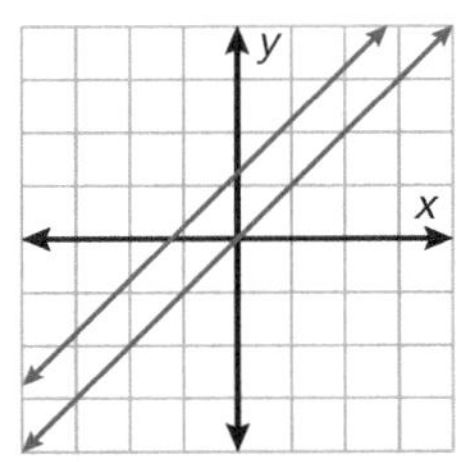
The graphed lines intersect at a single point.	The graphed lines are the same line. The line is the solution.	The lines are parallel and do not intersect.

Transformations of the Graph of $f(x) = \sqrt{x}$
Vertical translation: The graph of $f(x) = \sqrt{x} + c$ is c units up from the parent graph if $c > 0$ and the graph is c units down from the parent graph if $c < 0$.
Horizontal translation: The graph of $f(x) = \sqrt{x - c}$ is c units to the right of the parent graph if $c > 0$ and the graph is c units to the left of the parent graph if $c < 0$.

Reflections of the Graph of $f(x) = \sqrt{x}$
If $f(x) = \sqrt{x}$, then $g(x) = -\sqrt{x}$ is a reflection of the graph of f across the x-axis.
If $f(x) = \sqrt{x}$, then $g(x) = \sqrt{-x}$ is a reflection of the graph of f across the y-axis.

Functions and Relations

Arithmetic Sequence Formula
Use the formula below to find the next term in a sequence. $$a_n = a_{n-1} + d$$ $a_1 =$ first term $d =$ common difference $n =$ term number In the arithmetic sequence 7, 11, 15, 19, ..., $a_1 = 7$, $a_2 = 11$, $a_3 = 15$, and $a_4 = 19$. The common difference is 4.

Finding the nth Term of an Arithmetic Sequence
$$a_n = a_1 + (n - 1)d$$ $a_1 =$ first term $d =$ common difference

Finding the nth Term of a Geometric Sequence
Let $A(n)$ equal the nth term of a geometric sequence, then $$A(n) = ar^{n-1}$$ where a is the first term of the sequence and r is the common ratio.

Types of Graphs

Continuous Graph
A graph made up of connected lines or curves.

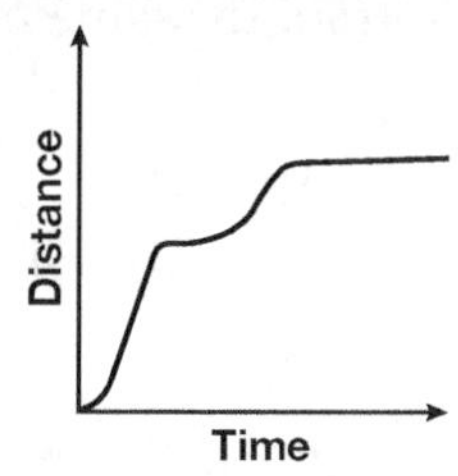

Discrete Graph
A graph made up of unconnected points.

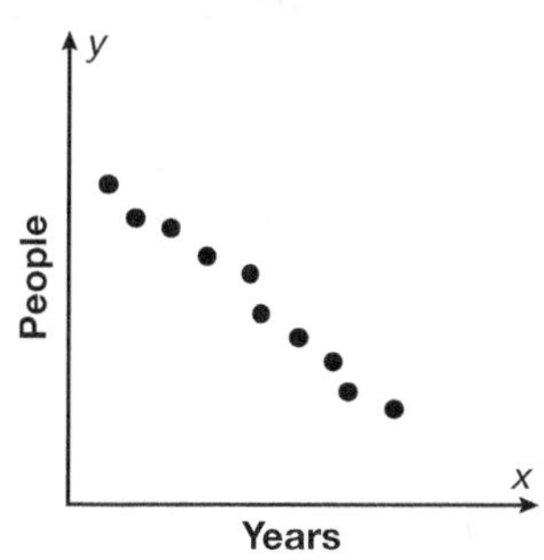

Equations and Inequalities

Graphing Inequalities on a Number Line			
Endpoint		**Arrow**	
$<, >, \neq$	$\leq, \geq$	$<, \leq$	$>, \geq$
open circle	closed circle	$\leftarrow$	$\rightarrow$
For $>$: Circle is open. Arrow points right. 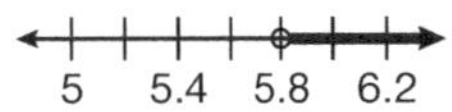		For $\leq$: Circle is closed. Arrow points left. 	

Addition and Subtraction Properties of Equality/Inequality
Addition Property of Equality You can add the same number to both sides of an equation and the statement will still be true. Examples: $2 = 2$ $3 + 2 = 2 + 3$ $5 = 5$ $a = b$ $a + c = b + c$ **Addition Property of Inequality** For any real numbers *a, b,* and *c:* If $a < b$, then $a + c < b + c$.   If $a \leq b$, then $a + c \leq b + c$. If $a > b$, then $a + c > b + c$.   If $a \geq b$, then $a + c \geq b + c$.
Subtraction Property of Equality You can subtract the same number from both sides of an equation and the statement will still be true. Examples: $10 = 10$ $10 - 4 = 10 - 4$ $6 = 6$ $a = b$ $a - c = b - c$ **Subtraction Property of Inequality** For any real numbers *a, b,* and *c:* If $a < b$, then $a - c < b - c$.   If $a \leq b$, then $a - c \leq b - c$. If $a > b$, then $a - c > b - c$.   If $a \geq b$, then $a - c \geq b - c$.

Equations and Inequalities

Multiplication Properties of Equality/Inequality
Multiplication Property of Equality Both sides of an equation can be multiplied by the same number, and the statement will still be true. Examples: $2 = 2$; $3 \cdot 2 = 3 \cdot 2$; $6 = 6$ — $a = b$; $a \cdot c = b \cdot c$; $ac = bc$
Multiplication Property of Inequality for $c < 0$ For every real number a and b, and $c < 0$: If $a > b$, then $ac < bc$. If $a < b$, then $ac > bc$. This property is also true for $\geq$ and $\leq$.

Division Properties of Equality/Inequality
Division Property of Equality Both sides of an equation can be divided by the same number, and the statement will still be true. Examples: $10 = 10$; $\frac{10}{2} = \frac{10}{2}$; $5 = 5$ — $a = b$; $\frac{a}{c} = \frac{b}{c} (c \neq 0)$
Division Property of Inequality for $c > 0$ For every real number a and b, and $c > 0$: If $a > b$, then $\frac{a}{c} > \frac{b}{c}$. If $a < b$, then $\frac{a}{c} < \frac{b}{c}$. This property is also true for $\geq$ and $\leq$.

Polynomials

Degrees of Expressions	
Degree of a Monomial	
The sum of the exponents of the variables in the monomial.	
$5x^2y^4z^3$	Degree: $2 + 4 + 3 = 9$
Degree of a Polynomial	
The degree of the term with the greatest degree.	
$2xy^2 + 3x^2y^4 + 6x^2y^2$	1st term degree: 3
2nd term degree: 6	3rd term degree: 4
Polynomial degree: 6	

The FOIL Method
First, Outer, Inner, Last
$(x + 2)(x + 3)$ First
$(x + 2)(x + 3)$ Outer
$(x + 2)(x + 3)$ Inner
$(x + 2)(x + 3)$ Last

Special Product of Binomials	
Square of a Binomial	
Pattern	**Example**
$(a + b)^2 = a^2 + 2ab + b^2$	$(x + 5)^2 = x^2 + 10x + 25$
$(a - b)^2 = a^2 - 2ab + b^2$	$(2x - 4)^2 = 4x^2 - 16x + 16$
Sum and Difference	
Pattern	**Example**
$(a + b)(a - b) = a^2 - b^2$	$(3x - 2)(3x + 2) = 9x^2 - 4$

Perfect-Square Trinomials	
The factored form of a perfect-square trinomial is:	
$a^2 + 2ab + b^2 = (a + b)^2$	Example: $x^2 + 12x + 36 = (x + 6)^2$
$a^2 - 2ab + b^2 = (a - b)^2$	Example: $x^2 - 12x + 36 = (x - 6)^2$

Probability and Data Analysis

Type of Events	Definition	Calculating the Probability
Independent Events	The outcome of the first event does not affect the second event.	$P(A \text{ and } B) = P(A) \cdot P(B)$
Dependent Events	The outcome of the first event does affect the second event.	$P(A \text{ and } B) = P(A) \cdot P(B)$, where $P(B)$ is calculated under the new conditions.

Probability of Mutually Exclusive Events
If A and B are mutually exclusive events, then $P(A \text{ or } B) = P(A) + P(B)$
Probability of Inclusive Events
If A and B are inclusive events, then $P(A \text{ or } B) = P(A) + P(B) - P(A \text{ and } B)$

Measures of Central Tendency	
Mean:	the average of a set of numbers
Median:	the middle number of a set of numbers arranged in order
Mode:	the number that appears the most often in a set of numbers
Range:	the difference between the least and the greatest numbers in a set of numbers

Stem-and-Leaf Plot

A graph used to organize and display data by dividing each data value into two parts, a stem and a leaf.

Stem	Leaves
2	2, 4, 5, 6
3	1, 2, 4
4	4, 7, 9

Key: 3|1 means 3.1

Box-and-Whisker Plot

The quartiles divide the data into fourths. The first quartile is the median of the lower half of the data, and the third quartile is the median of the upper half of the data.

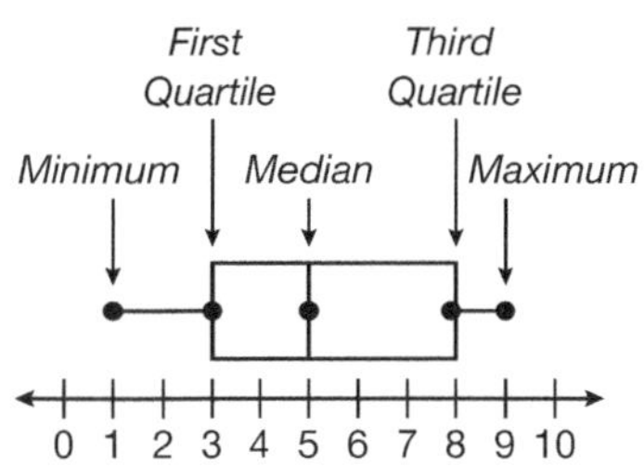

Frequency Distribution		
A table or graph that shows the number of observations falling into several ranges of data values	**Grade Range**	**Frequency (Number of Students)**
	0 to 40	3
	41 to 60	18
	61 to 80	27
	81 to 100	2

Scatter Plot Correlations

Strong positive correlation between x and y

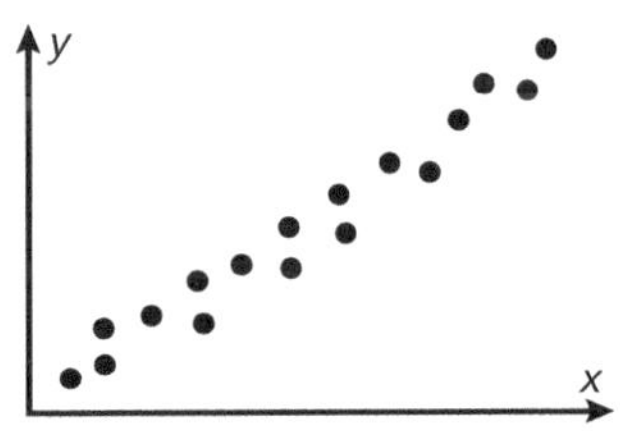

Strong negative correlation between x and y

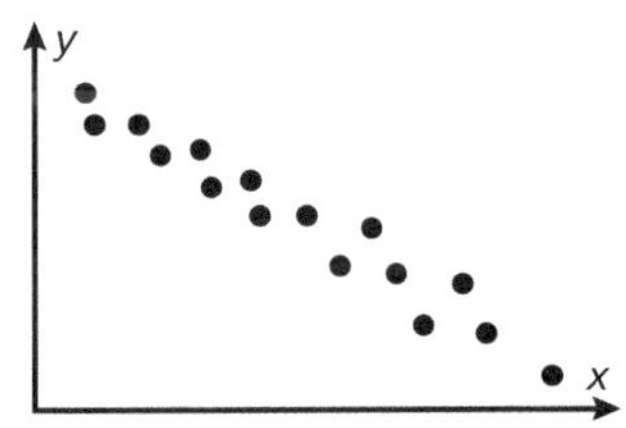

No correlation between x and y

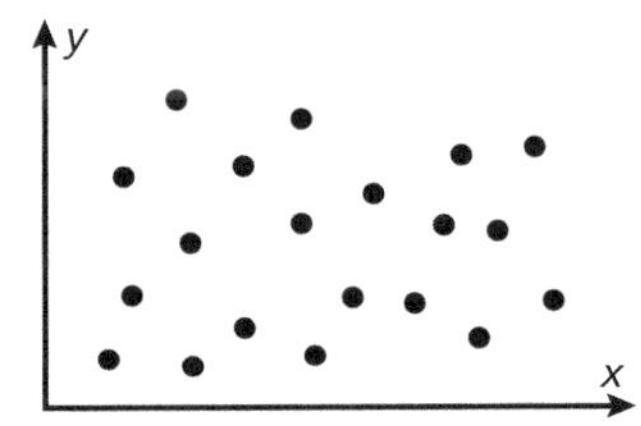

Trend Line

A line on a scatter plot that helps show the correlation between data sets more clearly is called a trend line or line of best fit.

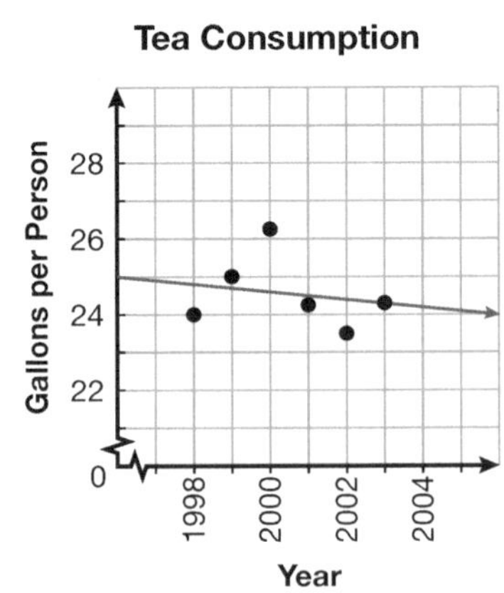

Geometry

Perimeter	
Rectangle	$P = 2l + 2w$ or $P = 2(l + w)$
Square	$P = 4s$

Circumference	
Circle	$C = \pi d$ or $C = 2\pi r$

Area	
Rectangle	$A = lw$
Triangle	$A = \frac{1}{2}bh$
Trapezoid	$A = \frac{1}{2}(b_1 + b_2)h$
Circle	$A = \pi r^2$

Surface Area	
Cube	$S = 6s^2$
Cylinder	$S = 2\pi r^2 + 2\pi rh$
Cone	$S = \pi r^2 + \pi rl$

Volume

Where B is the area of the base of a solid figure,

Prism or cylinder	$V = Bh$
Pyramid or cone	$V = \frac{1}{3}Bh$

Pythagorean Theorem

If a triangle is a right triangle with legs of lengths a and b and hypotenuse of length c, then

$$a^2 + b^2 = c^2.$$

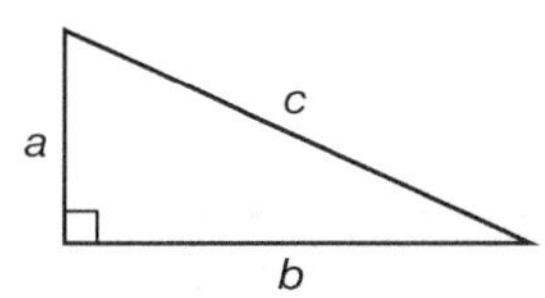

Converse of the Pythagorean Theorem

The **Converse of the Pythagorean Theorem** is also true; that is, if a triangle has side lengths a, b, and c that satisfy the equation $a^2 + b^2 = c^2$, then the triangle is a right triangle with legs of lengths a and b and hypotenuse of length c.

Sine, Cosine, and Tangent

$$\textbf{sine} \text{ of } \angle A = \frac{\text{length of leg opposite } \angle A}{\text{length of hypotenuse}} = \frac{a}{c}$$

$$\textbf{cosine} \text{ of } \angle A = \frac{\text{length of leg adjacent to } \angle A}{\text{length of hypotenuse}} = \frac{b}{c}$$

$$\textbf{tangent} \text{ of } \angle A = \frac{\text{length of leg opposite } \angle A}{\text{length of leg adjacent to } \angle A} = \frac{a}{b}$$

Geometry

Classifying Quadrilaterals	
Parallelogram Opposite sides are parallel and congruent. Opposite angles are congruent.	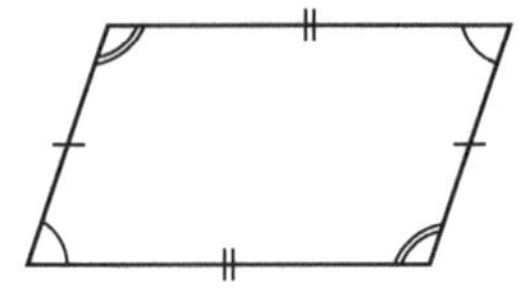
Rectangle Parallelogram with four right angles	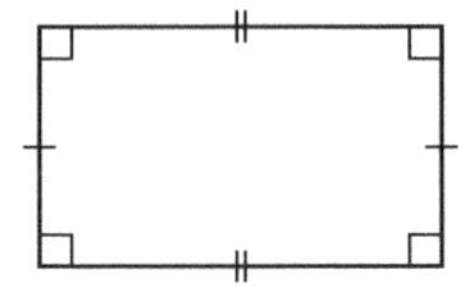
Rhombus Parallelogram with four congruent sides	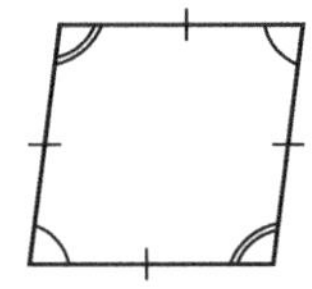
Square Rectangle with four congruent sides	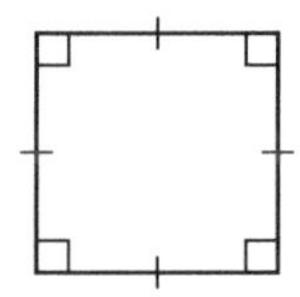
Trapezoid Quadrilateral with exactly two parallel sides May have two right angles	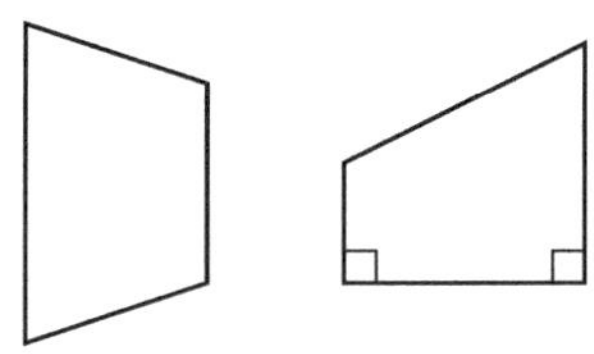

Classification of Angles			
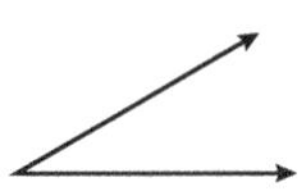	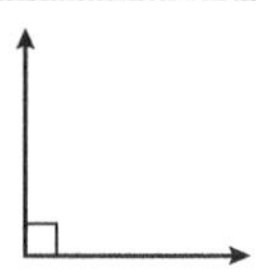	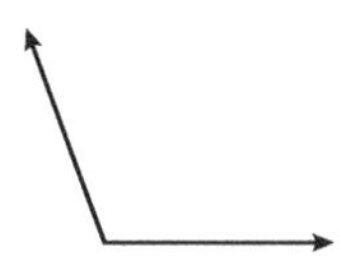	
An **acute angle** measures less than 90°.	A **right angle** measures exactly 90°.	An **obtuse angle** measures more than 90° and less than 180°.	A **straight angle** measures exactly 180°.

Geometry

Similar and Congruent Triangles	
Congruent Triangles	are the same shape and size. Angles and sides match. ($\triangle ABC$ and $\triangle DEF$)
Similar Triangles	are the same shape, have matching angles, but are not necessarily the same size. ($\triangle ABC$ and $\triangle GHI$)
Corresponding Angles	of similar triangles are the matching angles. ($\angle C$ and $\angle I$)
Corresponding Sides	of similar triangles are the sides opposite corresponding angles. ($\overline{AB}$ and $\overline{GH}$) The lengths of corresponding sides are proportional.

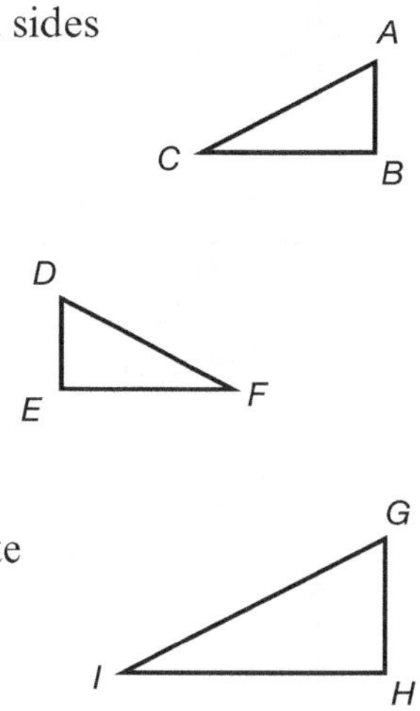

Classification of Triangles by Angle Measures

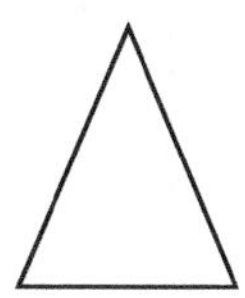

An **acute triangle** has three acute angles.

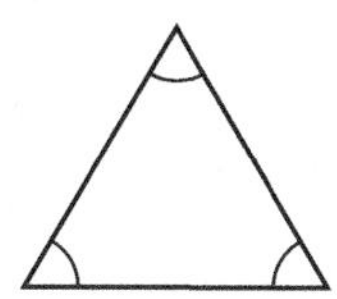

An **equiangular triangle** has three congruent acute angles.

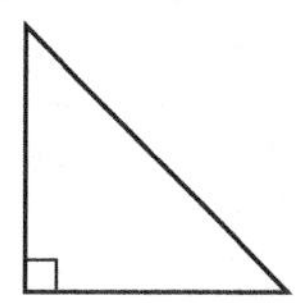

A **right triangle** has one right angle.

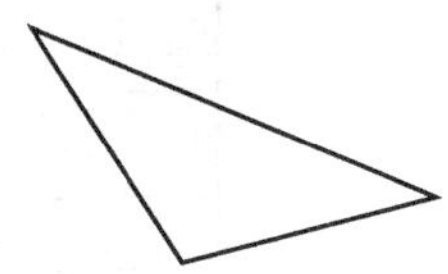

An **obtuse triangle** has one obtuse angle.

Classification of Triangles by Side Lengths

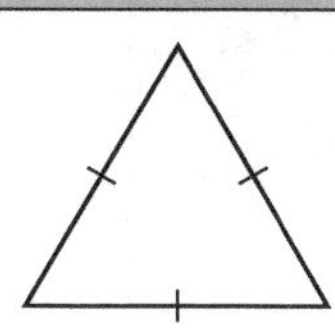

An **equilateral triangle** has three congruent sides.

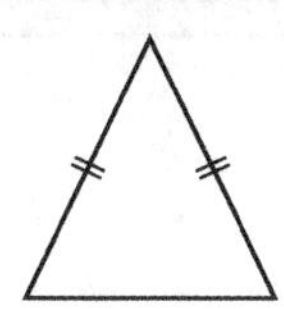

An **isosceles triangle** has at least two congruent sides.

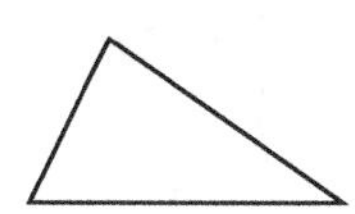

A **scalene triangle** has no congruent sides.

Measurement

Table of Metric Measures
Length
1 kilometer (km) = 1000 meters (m) 1 meter = 100 centimeters (cm) 1 centimeter = 10 millimeters (mm)
Capacity and Volume
1 liter (L) = 1000 milliliters (mL)
Mass
1 kilogram (kg) = 1000 grams (g)
Table of Customary Measures
Length
1 mile (mi) = 5280 feet (ft) 1 mile = 1760 yards (yd) 1 yard = 3 feet 1 yard = 36 inches (in.) 1 foot = 12 inches
Capacity and Volume
1 gallon (gal) = 4 quarts (qt) 1 quart = 2 pints (pt) 1 pint = 2 cups (c) 1 cup = 8 fluid ounces (fl oz)
Weight
1 ton = 2000 pounds (lb) 1 pound = 16 ounces (oz)
Customary and Metric Measures
1 inch = 2.54 centimeters 1 yard ≈ 0.9 meters 1 mile ≈ 1.6 kilometers
Time
1 year = 365 days 1 year = 12 months 1 month ≈ 4 weeks 1 year = 52 weeks 1 week = 7 days 1 day = 24 hours 1 hour (hr) = 60 minutes (min) 1 minute = 60 seconds (s)

Geometry Foundations

Name	Postulates/Theorems	Page
Postulate 1: Ruler Postulate	The points on a line can be paired in a one to one correspondence with the real numbers such that: **1.** any two given points can have coordinates 0 and 1. **2.** the distance between two points is the absolute value of the difference of their coordinates.	8
Postulate 2: Segment Addition Postulate	If B is between A and C, then $AB + BC = AC$.	9
Postulate 3: Protractor Postulate	Given a point, X, on $\overleftrightarrow{PR}$, consider $\overrightarrow{XP}$ and $\overrightarrow{XR}$, as well as all the other rays that can be drawn, with X as an endpoint, on one side of $\overleftrightarrow{PR}$. These rays can be paired with the real numbers from 0 to 180 such that: **1.** $\overrightarrow{XP}$ is paired with 0, and $\overrightarrow{XR}$ is paired with 180. **2.** If $\overrightarrow{XA}$ is paired with a number, c, and $\overrightarrow{XB}$ is paired with a number, d, then $m\angle AXB = \lvert c - d \rvert$.	14
Postulate 4: Angle Addition Postulate	If point D is in the interior of $\angle ABC$, then $m\angle ABD + m\angle DBC = m\angle ABC$.	15
Postulate 5	Through any two points there exists exactly one line.	21
Theorem 4-1	If two lines intersect, then they intersect at exactly one point.	21
Postulate 6	Through any three noncollinear points there exists exactly one plane.	22
Theorem 4-2	If there is a line and a point not on the line, then exactly one plane contains them.	22
Theorem 4-3	If two lines intersect, then there exists exactly one plane that contains them.	22
Postulate 7	If two planes intersect, then their intersection is a line.	23
Postulate 8	If two points lie in a plane, then the line containing the points lies in the plane.	23
Postulate 9	A line contains at least 2 points. A plane contains at least 3 noncollinear points. Space contains at least 4 noncoplanar points.	23
Theorem 5-1	If two parallel planes are cut by a third plane, then the lines of intersection are parallel.	27

GEOMETRY

Geometry Foundations

Name	Postulates/Theorems	Page
Theorem 5-2	If two lines in a plane are perpendicular to the same line, then they are parallel to each other.	28
Theorem 5-3	In a plane, if a line is perpendicular to one of two parallel lines, then it is perpendicular to the other one.	28
Theorem 5-4	If two lines are perpendicular, then they form congruent adjacent angles.	28
Theorem 5-5	If two lines form congruent adjacent angles, then they are perpendicular.	28
Theorem 5-6: Right Angles Theorem	All right angles are congruent.	28
Postulate 10: Parallel Postulate	Through a point not on a line, there exists exactly one line through the point parallel to the line.	29
Theorem 5-7: Transitive Property of Parallel Lines	If two lines are parallel to the same line, then they are parallel to each other.	29
Theorem 6-1: Congruent Complements Theorem	If two angles are complementary to the same angle or to congruent angles, then they are congruent.	35
Theorem 6-2: Congruent Supplements Theorem	If two angles are supplementary to the same angle or to congruent angles, then they are congruent.	35
Theorem 6-3: Linear Pair Theorem	If two angles form a linear pair, then they are supplementary.	36
Theorem 6-4: Vertical Angles Theorem	If two angles are vertical angles, then they are congruent.	36
Theorem 6-5	If a point lies on the perpendicular bisector of a segment, then the point is equidistant from the endpoints of the segment.	40
Theorem 6-6	If a point is equidistant from the endpoints of a segment, then the point lies on the perpendicular bisector of the segment.	40
Theorem 6-7	If a point lies on the bisector of an angle, then the point is equidistant from the sides of the angle.	41
Theorem 6-8	If a point is equidistant from the sides of an angle, then the point lies on the bisector of the angle.	41

Geometry Foundations

Name	Postulates/Theorems	Page
Postulate 11: Corresponding Angles Postulate	If two parallel lines are cut by a transversal, then the corresponding angles formed are congruent.	64
Theorem 10-1: Alternate Interior Angles Theorem	If two parallel lines are cut by a transversal, then the alternate interior angles are congruent.	64
Theorem 10-2: Alternate Exterior Angles Theorem	If two parallel lines are cut by a transversal, then the alternate exterior angles are congruent.	64
Theorem 10-3: Same-Side Interior Angles Theorem	If two parallel lines are cut by a transversal, then the same-side interior angles are supplementary.	65
Postulate 12: Converse of the Corresponding Angles Postulate	If two lines are cut by a transversal and the corresponding angles formed are congruent, then the lines are parallel.	71
Theorem 12-1: Converse of the Alternate Interior Angles Theorem	If two lines are cut by a transversal and the alternate interior angles are congruent, then the lines are parallel.	71
Theorem 12-2: Converse of the Alternate Exterior Angles Theorem	If two lines are cut by a transversal and the alternate exterior angles are congruent, then the lines are parallel.	72
Theorem 12-3: Converse of the Same-Side Interior Angles Theorem	If two lines are cut by a transversal and the same-side interior angles are supplementary, then the lines are parallel.	72
Theorem 60-3	If parallel lines intersect transversals, then they divide the transversals proportionally.	397
Theorem 60-4	If parallel lines cut congruent segments on one transversal, then they cut congruent segments on all transversals.	398

GEOMETRY

Geometry Foundations

Complementary Angles	Supplementary Angles
Two angles are **complementary angles** if the sum of their measures is 90°. $m\angle ABC + m\angle CBD = 90°$, so $\angle ABC$ is complementary to $\angle CBD$. 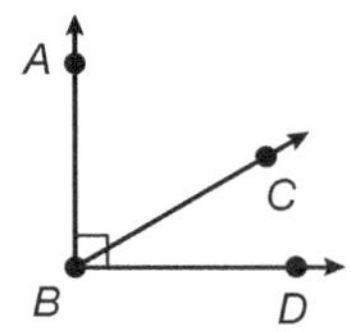 	Two angles are **supplementary angles** if the sum of their measures is 180°. $m\angle PQR + m\angle RQS = 180°$, so $\angle PQR$ is supplementary to $\angle RQS$. 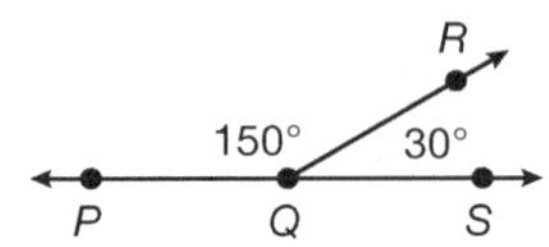

Classification	Example
A pair of **corresponding angles** is any pair of angles that lie on the same side of the transversal and on the same sides of the other two lines.	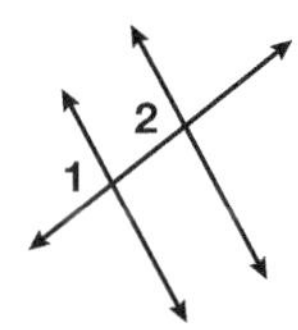
A pair of **alternate interior angles** is any pair of nonadjacent angles that lie on opposite sides of the transversal and between the other two lines.	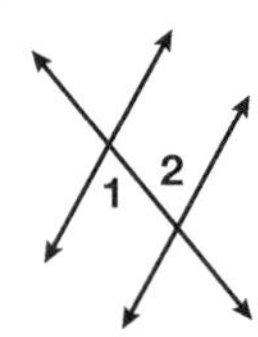
A pair of **alternate exterior angles** is any pair of angles that lie on opposite sides of the transversal and outside the other two lines.	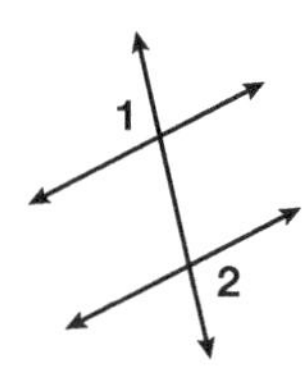
The **same-side interior angles,** also called the **consecutive interior angles,** are a pair of angles that lie on the same side of the transversal and between the other two lines.	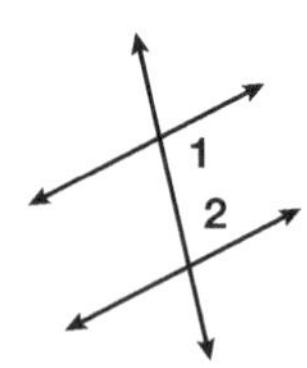

Substitution Property of Equality	If $a = b$, then b can be substituted for a in any expression.
Reflexive Property of Similarity	$\triangle ABC \sim \triangle ABC$
Reflexive Property of Congruence	$\overline{AB} \cong \overline{AB}$
Reflexive Property of Equality	$a = a$

Geometry Foundations

Symmetric Property of Similarity	If $\triangle ABC \sim \triangle DEF$, then $\triangle DEF \sim \triangle ABC$.
Symmetric Property of Congruence	If $\overline{AB} \cong \overline{CD}$, then $\overline{CD} \cong \overline{AB}$.
Symmetric Property of Equality	If $a = b$, then $b = a$.

Transitive Property of Similarity	If $\triangle ABC \sim \triangle DEF$ and $\triangle DEF \sim \triangle GHI$, then $\triangle ABC \sim \triangle GHI$.
Transitive Property of Congruence	If $\overline{AB} \cong \overline{CD}$ and $\overline{CD} \cong \overline{EF}$, then $\overline{AB} \cong \overline{EF}$.
Transitive Property of Equality	If $a = b$ and $b = c$, then $a = c$.

Area	
Rectangle	$A = bh$
Square	$A = s^2$
Rhombus	$A = \frac{1}{2}d_1d_2$
Parallelogram	$A = bh$
Triangle	$A = \frac{1}{2}bh$
Trapezoid	$A = \frac{1}{2}(b_1 + b_2)h$
Kite	$A = \frac{1}{2}d_1d_2$
Regular polygon	$A = \frac{1}{2}aP$

Circles	
Circumference	$C = 2\pi r$ or $C = \pi d$
Arc length	$L = 2\pi r\left(\frac{m^\circ}{360^\circ}\right)$
Area	$A = \pi r^2$
Area of a sector	$A = \pi r^2\left(\frac{m^\circ}{360^\circ}\right)$
Area of a circle segment	$A_{segment} = A_{sector} - A_{triangle}$
Equation of a circle	$(x - h)^2 + (y - k)^2 = r^2$

Lateral Area	
Prism	$L = Ph$
Cylinder	$L = 2\pi rh$
Pyramid	$L = \frac{1}{2}Pl$
Cone	$L = \pi rl$

Surface Area	
Cube	$S = 6s^2$
Cylinder	$S = 2\pi r^2 + 2\pi rh$
Cone	$S = \pi r^2 + \pi rl$
Prism	$S = L + 2B$
Pyramid	$S = L + B$
Sphere	$S = 4\pi r^2$

Volume	
Prism	$V = \text{Bh}$
Cylinder	$V = \pi r^2 h$
Pyramid or cone	$V = \frac{1}{3}Bh$
Sphere	$V = \frac{4}{3}\pi r^3$
Frustum of a cone	$V = \frac{1}{3}h(B_1 + \sqrt{B_1B_2} + B_2)$

GEOMETRY

Triangles, Congruence, and Similarity

Name	Postulates/Theorems	Page
Theorem 18-1: Triangle Sum Theorem	The sum of the measures of the angles of a triangle is equal to 180°.	109
Corollary 18-1-1: Third Angle Theorem	If two angles of one triangle are congruent to two angles of another triangle, then the third angles are congruent.	110
Corollary 18-1-2	The acute angles of a right triangle are complementary.	110
Corollary 18-1-3	The measure of each angle of an equiangular triangle is 60°.	110
Corollary 18-1-4	A triangle can have at most one right or one obtuse angle.	110
Theorem 18-2: Exterior Angle Theorem	The measure of each exterior angle of a triangle is equal to the sum of the measures of its two remote interior angles.	111
Postulate 13: Side-Side-Side (SSS) Triangle Congruence Postulate	If three sides of one triangle are congruent to three sides of another triangle, then the triangles are congruent.	158
Postulate 15: Side-Angle-Side (SAS) Triangle Congruence Postulate	If two sides and the included angle of one triangle are congruent to two sides and the included angle of another triangle, then the triangles are congruent.	175
Postulate 16: Angle-Side-Angle (ASA) Triangle Congruence Postulate	If two angles and the included side of one triangle are congruent to two angles and the included side of another triangle, then the triangles are congruent.	188
Theorem 30-1: Angle-Angle-Side (AAS) Triangle Congruence Theorem	If two angles and a non-included side of one triangle are congruent to two angles and the corresponding non-included side of another triangle, then the triangles are congruent.	189
Theorem 32-1: Centroid Theorem	The centroid of a triangle is located $\frac{2}{3}$ the distance from each vertex to the midpoint of the opposite side.	205

Triangles, Congruence, and Similarity

Name	Postulates/Theorems	Page
Theorem 38-1: Triangle Angle Bisector Theorem	If a line bisects an angle of a triangle, then it divides the opposite side proportionally to the other two sides of the triangle.	245
Theorem 39-1	If one side of a triangle is longer than another side, then the angle opposite the first side is larger than the angle opposite the second side.	251
Theorem 39-2	If one angle of a triangle is larger than another angle, then the side opposite the first angle is longer than the side opposite the second angle.	251
Theorem 39-3: Exterior Angle Inequality Theorem	The measure of an exterior angle of a triangle is greater than the measure of either remote interior angle.	252
Theorem 39-4: Triangle Inequality Theorem	The sum of the lengths of any two sides of a triangle must be greater than the length of the third side.	252
Theorem 40-1: Hinge Theorem	If two sides of one triangle are congruent to two sides of another triangle and the included angle of the first triangle is greater than the included angle of the second triangle, then the third side of the first triangle is longer than the third side of the second triangle.	263
Theorem 40-2: Converse of the Hinge Theorem	If two sides of one triangle are congruent to two sides of another triangle and the third side of the first triangle is longer than the third side of the second triangle, then the measure of the angle opposite the third side of the first triangle is greater than the measure of the angle opposite the third side of the second triangle.	264
Postulate 21: Angle-Angle (AA) Triangle Similarity Postulate	If two angles of one triangle are congruent to two angles of another triangle, then the triangles are similar.	301
Theorem 46-1: Side-Side-Side (SSS) Similarity Theorem	If the lengths of the sides of a triangle are proportional to the lengths of the sides of another triangle, then the triangles are similar.	302

GEOMETRY

Triangles, Congruence, and Similarity

Name	Postulates/Theorems	Page
Theorem 46-2: Side-Angle-Side (SAS) Similarity Theorem	If two sides of one triangle are proportional to two sides of another triangle and the included angles are congruent, then the triangles are similar.	303
Theorem 51-1: Isosceles Triangle Theorem	If a triangle is isosceles, then its base angles are congruent.	336
Corollary 51-1-1	If a triangle is equilateral, then it is equiangular.	336
Theorem 51-2: Converse of the Isosceles Triangle Theorem	If two angles of a triangle are congruent, then the sides opposite those angles are also congruent.	337
Corollary 51-2-1	If a triangle is equiangular, then it is equilateral.	337
Theorem 51-3	If a line bisects the vertex angle in an isosceles triangle, then it is the perpendicular bisector of the base.	338
Theorem 51-4	If a line is the perpendicular bisector of the base of an isosceles triangle, then it bisects the vertex angle.	338
Theorem 55-1: Triangle Midsegment Theorem	The segment joining the midpoints of two sides of a triangle is parallel to, and half the length of, the third side.	361
Theorem 55-2	If a line is parallel to one side of a triangle and it contains the midpoint of another side, then it passes through the midpoint of the third side.	362
Theorem 60-1: Triangle Proportionality Theorem	If a line parallel to one side of a triangle intersects the other two sides, then it divides those sides proportionally.	396
Theorem 60-2: Converse of the Triangle Proportionality Theorem	If a line divides two sides of a triangle proportionally, then it is parallel to the third side.	397

CPCTC
An abbreviation of the phrase "**C**orresponding **P**arts of **C**ongruent **T**riangles are **C**ongruent."

Triangles, Congruence, and Similarity

Centers of a Triangle		
Centroid	The point of concurrency of the three medians of a triangle. It is $\frac{2}{3}$ the distance from each vertex to the midpoint of the opposite side.	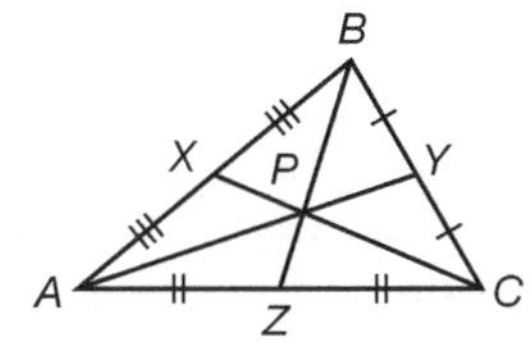
Circumcenter	The point of concurrency of the three perpendicular bisectors of a triangle. It is equidistant from the sides of the triangle.	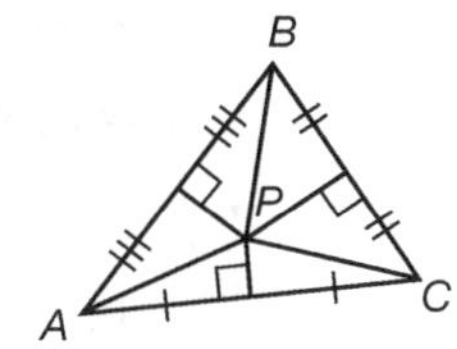
Incenter	The point of concurrency of the three angle bisectors of a triangle.	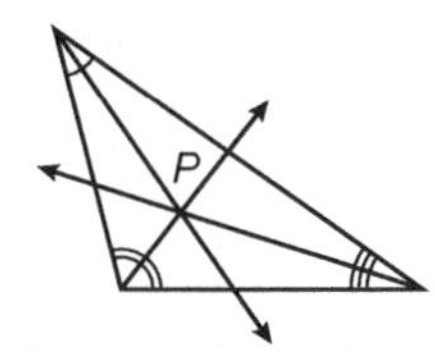
Orthocenter	The altitude of a triangle is a perpendicular segment from a vertex to the line containing the opposite side. The orthocenter of a triangle is the point of concurrency of the three altitudes of a triangle.	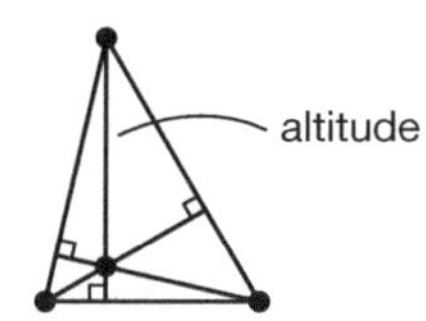

GEOMETRY

Circles

Name	Postulates/Theorems	Page
Postulate 14: Arc Addition Postulate	The measure of an arc formed by two adjacent arcs is the sum of the measures of the two arcs.	164
Theorem 43-1	If a diameter is perpendicular to a chord, then it bisects the chord and its arcs.	282
Theorem 43-2	If a diameter bisects a chord other than another diameter, then it is perpendicular to the chord.	282
Theorem 43-3	The perpendicular bisector of a chord contains the center of the circle.	283

Circles

Name	Postulates/Theorems	Page
Theorem 43-4	In a circle or congruent circles (1) chords equidistant from the center are congruent (2) congruent chords are equidistant from the center of the circle.	283
Theorem 47-1	The measure of an inscribed angle is equal to half the measure of its intercepted arc.	308
Theorem 47-2	If an inscribed angle intercepts a semicircle, then it is a right angle.	308
Theorem 47-3	If two inscribed angles intercept the same arc, then they are congruent.	310
Theorem 47-4	If a quadrilateral is inscribed in a circle, then it has supplementary opposite angles.	310
Theorem 58-1	If a line is tangent to a circle, then the line is perpendicular to a radius drawn to the point of tangency.	381
Theorem 58-2	If a line in the plane of a circle is perpendicular to a radius at its endpoint on the circle, then the line is tangent to the circle.	382
Theorem 58-3	If two tangent segments are drawn to a circle from the same exterior point, then they are congruent.	383
Theorem 64-1	The measure of an angle formed by a tangent and a chord is equal to half the measure of the intercepted arc.	424
Theorem 64-2	The measure of an angle formed by two chords intersecting in a circle is equal to half the sum of the intercepted arcs.	425
Theorem 79-1	The measure of an angle whose vertex is outside a circle is equal to half the difference of the intercepted arcs.	518
Theorem 86-1	If two chords intersect in a circle, then the products of the chord segments are equal.	560
Theorem 101-1	If two secant segments are drawn through a circle from an external point, then the product of one secant segment and its external segment is equal to the product of the other secant segment and its external segment.	656
Theorem 101-2	If a secant segment and a tangent segment are drawn through a circle from an external point, then the product of the length of the secant segment and its external segment is equal to the length of the tangent segment squared.	657
Theorem 104-1	In the same or congruent circles (1) congruent arcs have congruent chords (2) congruent chords have congruent arcs.	674

Polygons

Name	Postulates/Theorems	Page
Postulate 19: Area Congruence Postulate	If two polygons are congruent, then they have the same area.	257
Postulate 20: Area Addition Postulate	The area of a region is equal to the sum of the areas of its non-overlapping parts.	257
Theorem 44-1	If two polygons are similar, then the ratio of their perimeters is equal to the ratio of their corresponding sides.	289
Theorem 69-1: Trapezoid Midsegment Theorem	The midsegment of a trapezoid is parallel to both bases and has a length that is equal to half the sum of the bases.	457
Theorem 87-1	If two similar figures have a scale factor of $a{:}b$, then the ratio of their perimeters is $a{:}b$, and the ratio of their areas is $a^2{:}b^2$.	567

Properties of Isosceles Trapezoids	
Base angles of an isosceles trapezoid are congruent. If trapezoid $HIJK$ is isosceles, then $\angle H \cong \angle I$, and $\angle J \cong \angle K$.	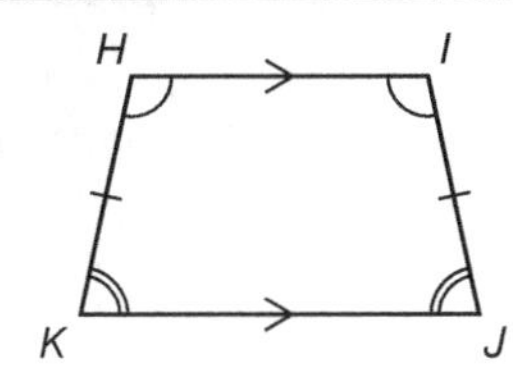
The diagonals of an isosceles trapezoid are congruent. In isosceles trapezoid $STUV$, $\overline{SU} \cong \overline{TV}$.	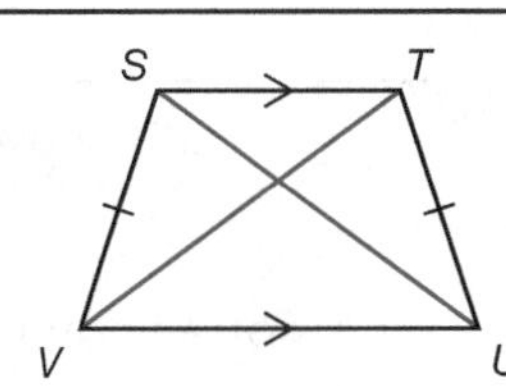

Properties of Kites	
The diagonals of a kite are perpendicular. $\overline{EG} \perp \overline{FH}$	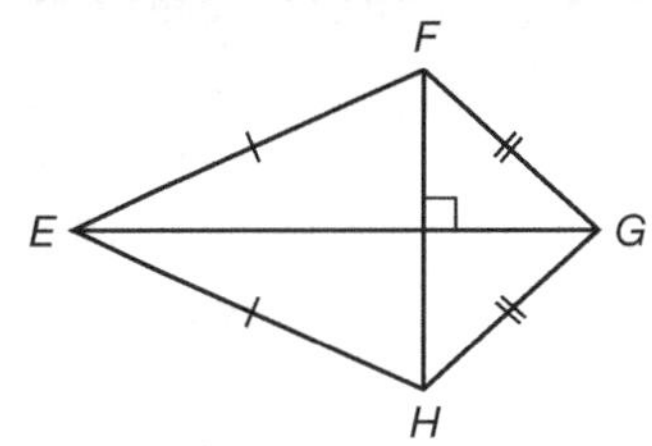

GEOMETRY

Polygons

Properties of Parallelograms	
1. If a quadrilateral is a parallelogram, then its opposite angles are congruent. $\angle J \cong \angle L$ $\angle M \cong \angle K$	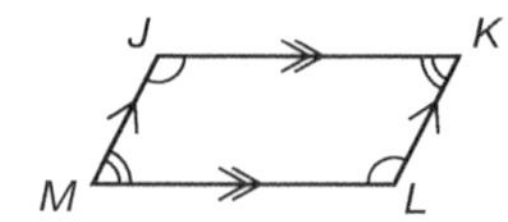
2. If a quadrilateral is a parallelogram, then its consecutive angles are supplementary. $m\angle S + m\angle T = 180°$ $m\angle T + m\angle U = 180°$ $m\angle U + m\angle V = 180°$ $m\angle V + m\angle S = 180°$	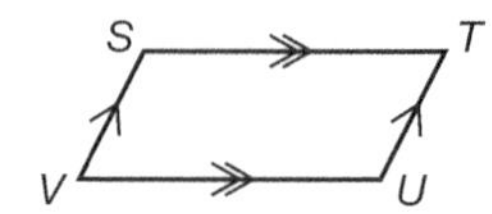
3. If a quadrilateral is a parallelogram, then its opposite sides are congruent. $\overline{AD} \cong \overline{BC}$ $\overline{AB} \cong \overline{DC}$	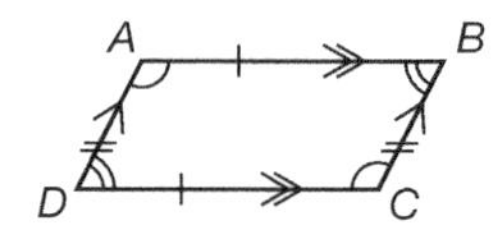
4. If a quadrilateral is a parallelogram, then its diagonals bisect each other. $NE = EP$ $QE = EO$	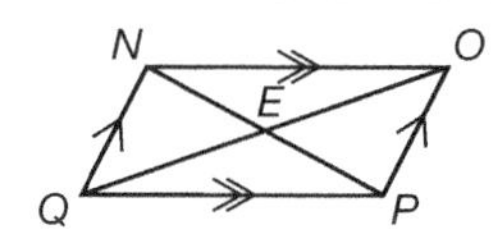

Properties of a Rectangle: Congruent Diagonals	
The diagonals of a rectangle are congruent. $\overline{PR} \cong \overline{QS}$	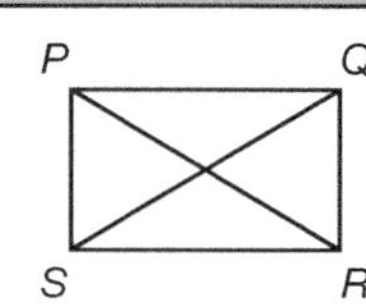

Properties of a Rhombus: Perpendicular Diagonals	
The diagonals of a rhombus are perpendicular. $\overline{HJ} \perp \overline{IK}$	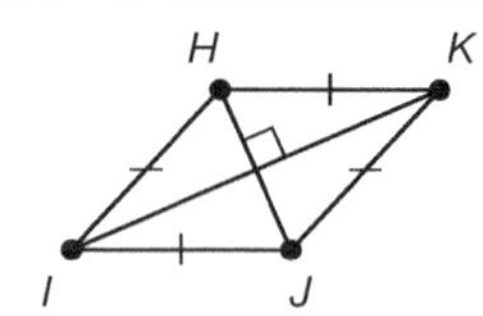

Properties of a Rhombus: Diagonals as Angle Bisectors	
Each diagonal of a rhombus bisects opposite angles. Because opposite angles of a rhombus are equal, when they are bisected by a diagonal, four congruent angles result. $\angle 1 \cong \angle 2 \cong \angle 5 \cong \angle 6$, and $\angle 3 \cong \angle 4 \cong \angle 7 \cong \angle 8$	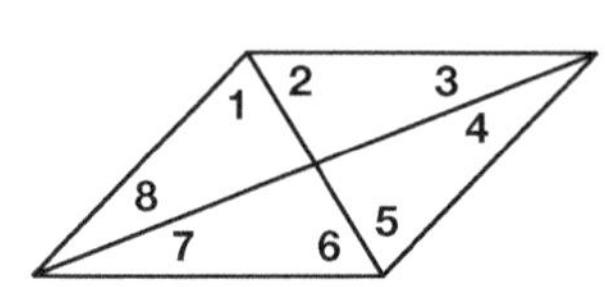

Polygons

Classifying Polygons			
Name	**Sides**	**Regular Polygon**	**Irregular Polygon**
Triangle	3	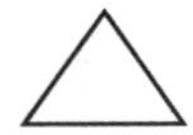	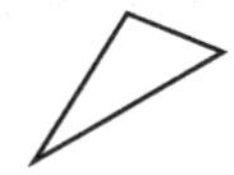
Quadrilateral	4	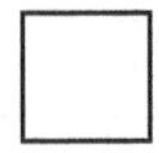	
Pentagon	5	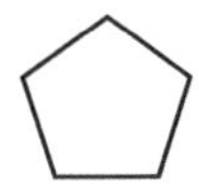	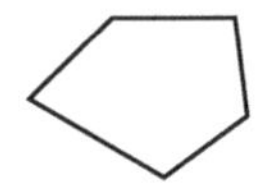
Hexagon	6		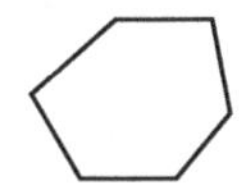
Heptagon	7		
Octagon	8		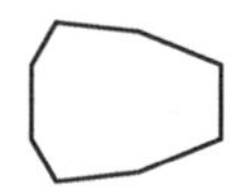
Nonagon	9		
Decagon	10	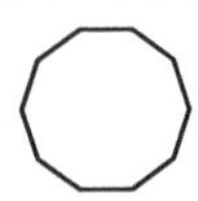	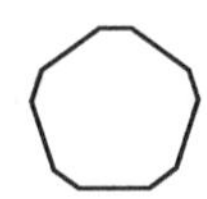
Hendecagon	11		
Dodecagon	12	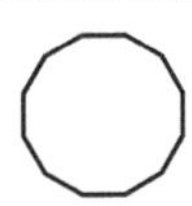	

Tessellations	
A repeating pattern of plane figures that completely covers a plane with no gaps or overlaps.	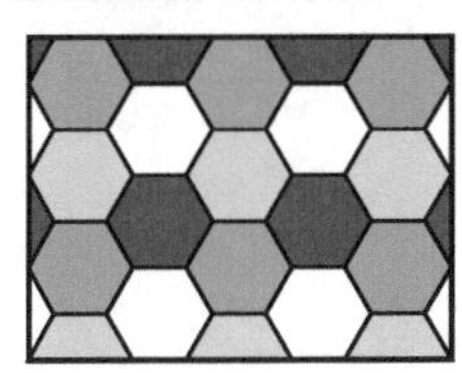

GEOMETRY

Polygons

Formula for the Sum of the Interior Angles of a Polygon
To find the sum of the interior angles of a polygon, use the formula below, where n is the number of sides of the polygon. $$(n - 2)180^\circ$$

Formula for Interior Angle Measure of a Regular Polygon	
To find the measure of each interior angle, use the formula below, where n is the number of sides of the polygon. $$\frac{(n - 2)180^\circ}{n}$$	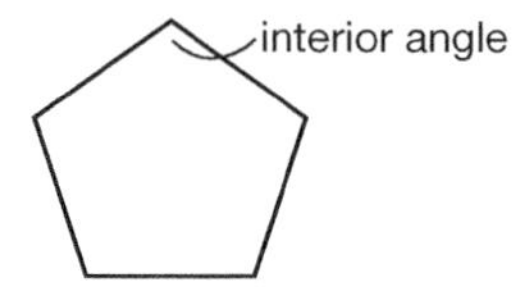

Formula for Exterior Angle Measure of a Regular Polygon	
To find the exterior angle measures of a regular polygon, use the formula below, where n is the number of sides in the polygon. $$\frac{360^\circ}{n}$$	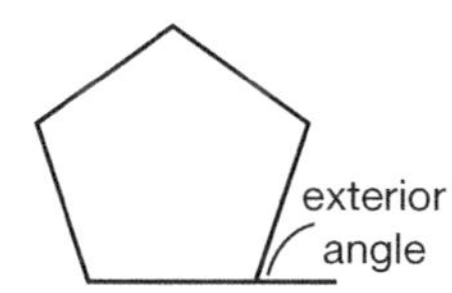

Formula for Central Angle Measure of a Regular Polygon	
To find the measure of each central angle of a regular polygon, use the formula below, where n is the number of sides in the polygon. $$\frac{360^\circ}{n}$$	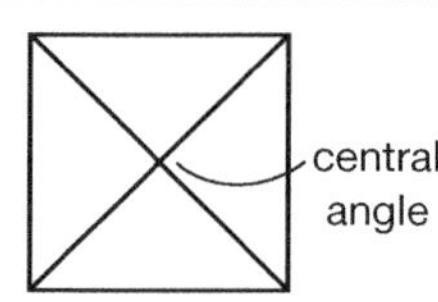

Right Triangles and Trigonometry

Name	Postulates/Theorems	Page
Theorem 33-1: Converse of the Pythagorean Theorem	If the sum of the squares of the two shorter sides of a triangle is equal to the square of the longest side of the triangle, then the triangle is a right triangle.	212
Theorem 33-2: Pythagorean Inequality Theorem	In a triangle, let a and b be the lengths of the two shorter sides and let c be the length of the longest side. If $a^2 + b^2 < c^2$, then the triangle is obtuse. If $a^2 + b^2 > c^2$, then the triangle is acute.	213
Theorem 36-1: Leg-Angle (LA) Right Triangle Congruence Theorem	If a leg and an acute angle of one right triangle are congruent to a leg and an acute angle of another right triangle, then the triangles are congruent.	230
Theorem 36-2: Hypotenuse-Angle (HA) Right Triangle Congruence Theorem	If the hypotenuse and an acute angle of one right triangle are congruent to the hypotenuse and an acute angle of another right triangle, then the triangles are congruent.	231
Theorem 36-3: Leg-Leg (LL) Right Triangle Congruence Theorem	If the two legs of one right triangle are congruent to the two legs of another right triangle, then the triangles are congruent.	231
Theorem 36-4: Hypotenuse-Leg (HL) Right Triangle Congruence Theorem	If the hypotenuse and a leg of one right triangle are congruent to the hypotenuse and a leg of another right triangle, then the triangles are congruent.	232
Theorem 50-1	If the altitude is drawn to the hypotenuse of a right triangle, then the two triangles formed are similar to each other and to the original triangle.	327
Corollary 50-1-1	If the altitude is drawn to the hypotenuse of a right triangle, then the length of the altitude is the geometric mean between the segments of the hypotenuse.	329
Corollary 50-1-2	If the altitude is drawn to the hypotenuse of a right triangle, then the length of a leg is the geometric mean between the hypotenuse and the segment of the hypotenuse that is closer to that leg.	329

Right Triangles and Trigonometry

Geometric Mean	
For positive numbers a and b, the positive number x such that $\frac{a}{x} = \frac{x}{b}$.	$\frac{a}{x} = \frac{x}{b}$ $x^2 = ab$ $x = \sqrt{ab}$

Properties of a 45°-45°-90° Triangle: Side Lengths	
In a 45°-45°-90° right triangle, both legs are congruent and the length of the hypotenuse is the length of a leg multiplied by $\sqrt{2}$.	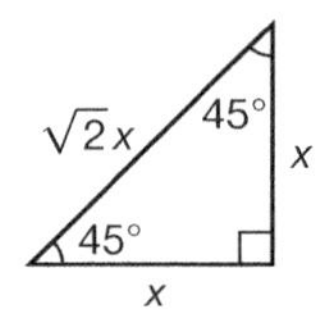

Properties of 30°-60°-90° Triangles	
In a 30°-60°-90° triangle, the length of the hypotenuse is twice the length of the short leg, and the length of the longer leg is the length of the shorter leg times $\sqrt{3}$.	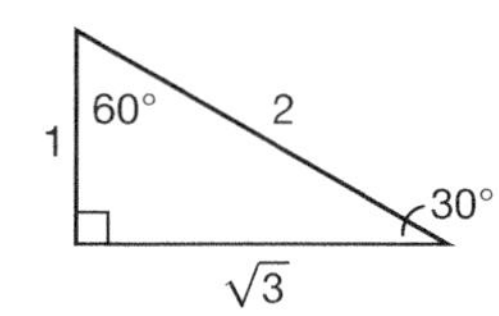

Law of Cosines
In any triangle ABC: $a^2 = b^2 + c^2 - 2bc \cos A$ $b^2 = a^2 + c^2 - 2ac \cos B$ $c^2 = a^2 + b^2 - 2ab \cos C$.

Law of Sines
In any triangle ABC: $\frac{a}{\sin A} = \frac{b}{\sin B} = \frac{c}{\sin C}$.

Angles of Depression/Elevation	
angle of depression The angle formed by a horizontal line and a line of sight to a point below.	
angle of elevation The angle formed by a horizontal line and a line of sight to a point above.	

Coordinate Geometry

Name	Postulates/Theorems	Page
Postulate 17: Parallel Lines Postulate	If two lines are parallel, then they have the same slope. All vertical lines are parallel to each other.	237
Postulate 18: Perpendicular Lines Postulate	If two nonvertical lines are perpendicular, then the product of their slopes is -1. Vertical and horizontal lines are perpendicular to each other.	237
Theorem 42-1	Through a line and a point not on the line, there exists exactly one perpendicular line to the given line.	274
Theorem 42-2	The perpendicular segment from a point to a line is the shortest segment from the point to the line.	275
Theorem 42-3	The perpendicular segment from a point to a plane is the shortest segment from the point to the plane.	397
Theorem 42-4	If two lines are parallel, then all points on one line are equidistant from the other line.	398

Quadrants on a Coordinate Plane

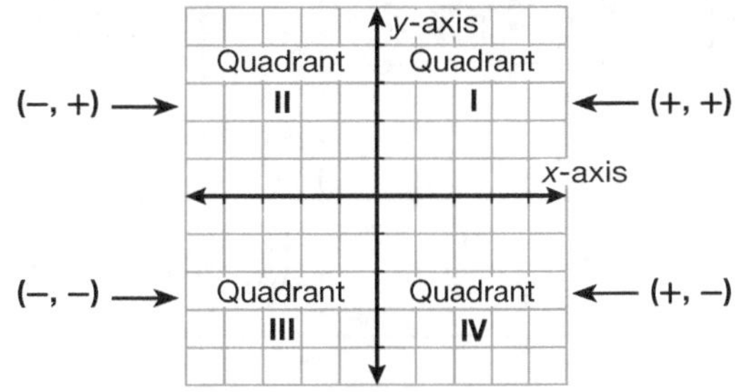

Properties of Isometries and Transformations

- An isometry maps a figure to a congruent figure.
- A translation is an isometry.
- A reflection is an isometry.
- A rotation is an isometry.
- A dilation maps a figure to a similar figure.
- The composition of two isometries is an isometry.
- The composition of two reflections across two parallel lines is a translation.
- The composition of two reflections across two intersecting lines is a rotation about the point of intersection. The angle of rotation is twice the angle formed by the intersecting lines.

GEOMETRY

Coordinate Geometry

Rotation Matrices and Associated Mappings		
For points rotated about the origin:		
Degrees	**Rotation Matrix**	**Mapping**
90°	$\begin{bmatrix} 0 & -1 \\ 1 & 0 \end{bmatrix}$	$(x, y) \longrightarrow (-y, x)$
180°	$\begin{bmatrix} -1 & 0 \\ 0 & -1 \end{bmatrix}$	$(x, y) \longrightarrow (-x, -y)$
270°	$\begin{bmatrix} 0 & 1 \\ -1 & 0 \end{bmatrix}$	$(x, y) \longrightarrow (y, -x)$
360°	$\begin{bmatrix} 1 & 0 \\ 0 & 1 \end{bmatrix}$	$(x, y) \longrightarrow (x, y)$

Reflection Matrices and Associated Mappings		
For points reflected over an axis:		
	Reflection Matrix	**Mapping**
x-axis	$\begin{bmatrix} 1 & 0 \\ 0 & -1 \end{bmatrix}$	$(x, y) \longrightarrow (x, -y)$
y-axis	$\begin{bmatrix} -1 & 0 \\ 0 & 1 \end{bmatrix}$	$(x, y) \longrightarrow (-x, y)$

Coordinate Geometry

Determinant of an $m \times 2$ Matrix Used for Finding Area
Given $A = \begin{bmatrix} x_1 & y_1 \\ x_2 & y_2 \\ x_3 & y_3 \\ \vdots & \vdots \\ x_m & y_m \end{bmatrix}$, the determinant of A is given by the formula:
$\det(A) = (x_1y_2 + x_2y_3 + x_3y_4 + \ldots + x_my_1 - y_1x_2 - y_2x_3 - y_3x_4 - \ldots - y_mx_1)$

Matrix Method of Computing Area of a Polygon
Given a convex polygon with n vertices, (x_1, y_1), (x_2, y_2), up to (x_n, y_n), the area of the polygon is equal to the absolute value of one-half of the determinant of the matrix listing the coordinates vertically.
$A = \left\lvert \frac{1}{2}\det\begin{bmatrix} x_1 & y_1 \\ x_2 & y_2 \\ \vdots & \vdots \\ x_m & y_m \end{bmatrix} \right\rvert$
So, the area of the polygon can be given by the formula.
$A = \left\lvert \frac{1}{2}(x_1y_2 + x_2y_3 + x_3y_4 + \ldots + x_ny_1 - y_1x_2 - y_2x_3 - y_3x_4 - \ldots - y_nx_1) \right\rvert$

GEOMETRY

Solids

Solids	
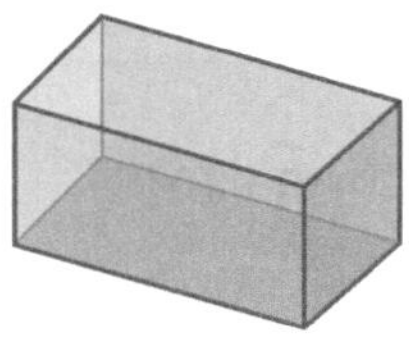 polyhedron	Any closed three-dimensional figure formed by four or more polygons that intersect only at their edges is called a polyhedron.
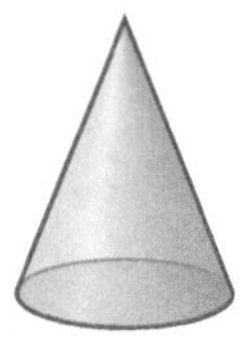 cone	A cone is a three-dimensional figure with a circular base and a curved lateral surface that comes to a point.
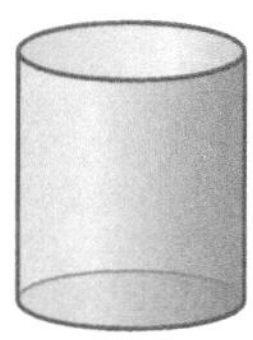 cylinder	A cylinder is a three-dimensional figure with two parallel circular bases and a curved lateral surface that connects the bases.
 sphere	A sphere is the set of points in space that are a fixed distance from a given point, called the center of the sphere.
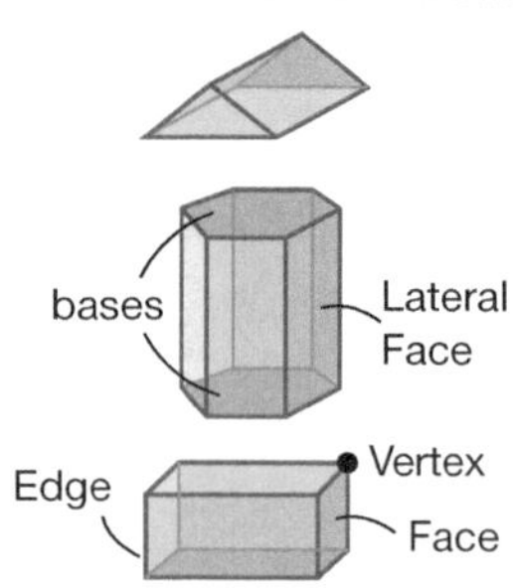	A prism is a polyhedron formed by two parallel congruent polygonal bases connected by lateral faces that are parallelograms. The base of a prism is one of the two congruent parallel faces of the prism. A face of a prism that is not a base is called a lateral face.
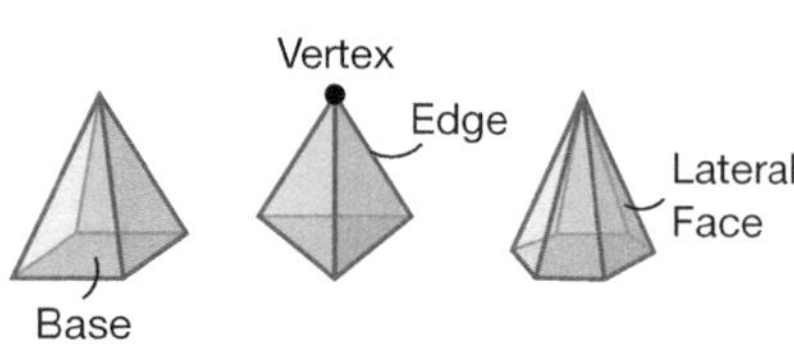	A pyramid is a polyhedron formed by a polygonal base and triangular lateral faces that meet at a common vertex. The faces of a pyramid all share a common vertex. The base is the side of the pyramid that does not share a single vertex with all of the other sides.

Solids

Euler's Formula
For any polyhedron with V vertices, E edges and F faces, $V - E + F = 2$.

Cavalieri's Principle
If two solids lying between parallel planes have equal heights and all cross sections at equal distances from their bases have equal areas, then the solids have equal volumes.

GEOMETRY

Logic and Reasoning

Logic Terms	
conjecture	A statement that is believed to be true.
counterexample	An example that proves a conjecture or statement is false.
tautology	A logic statement that is always true.
contradiction	A logic statement that is always false.

Truth Table		
Hypothesis: p	**Conclusion: q**	**Statement: If p, then q**
T	T	T
T	F	F
F	T	T
F	F	T

Types of Conditional Statements	
Type	**Form**
Statement	If p, then q
Converse	If q, then p
Inverse	If $\sim p$, then $\sim q$
Contrapositive	If $\sim q$, then $\sim p$

Law of Detachment
For two statements p and q, when "If p, then q" is a true statement and p is true, then q is true.

Law of Syllogism
When "If p, then q" and "If q, then r" are true statements, then "If p, then r" is a true statement.

Linear/Quadratic Functions

Types of Functions

Continuous Functions

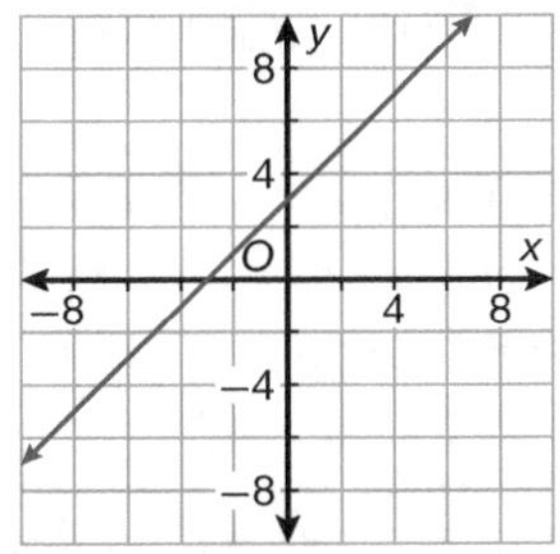

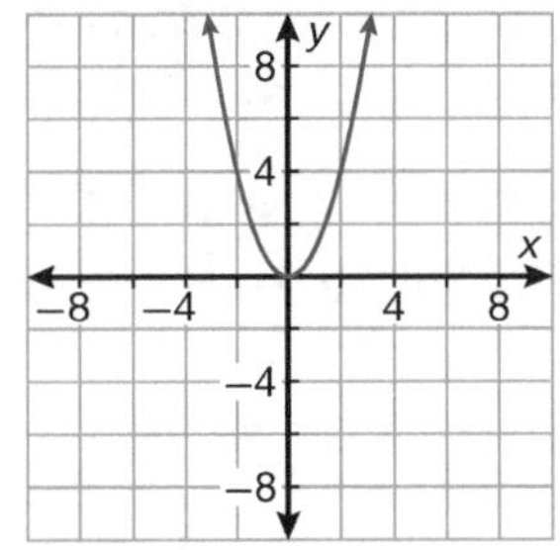

Discontinuous Functions

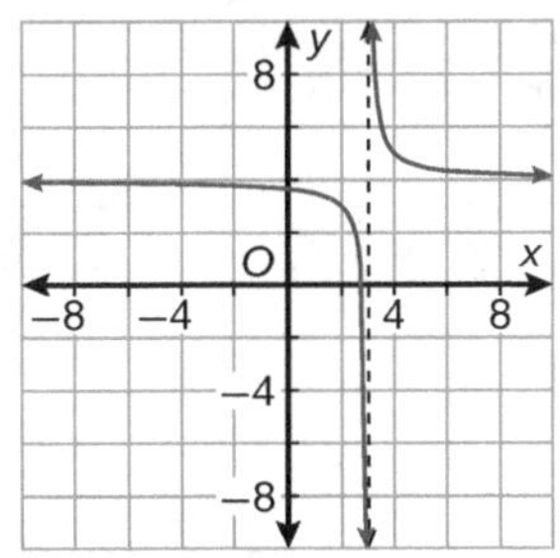

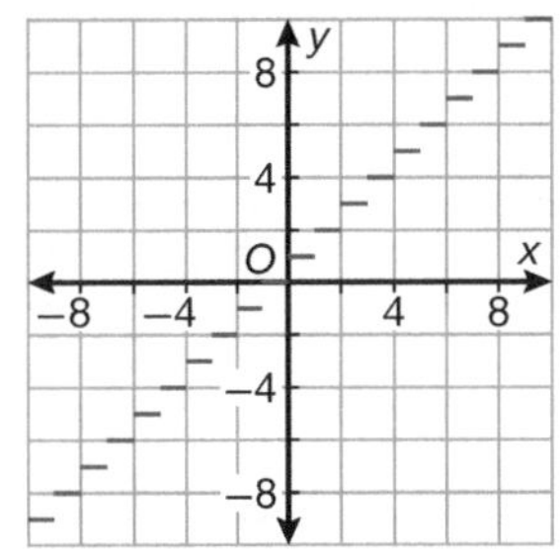

Discrete Functions

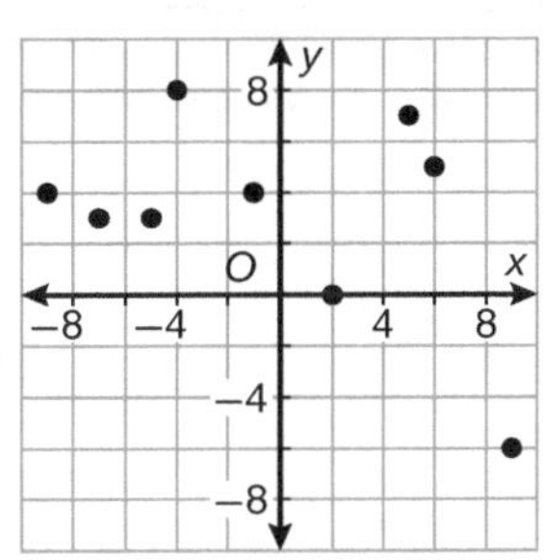

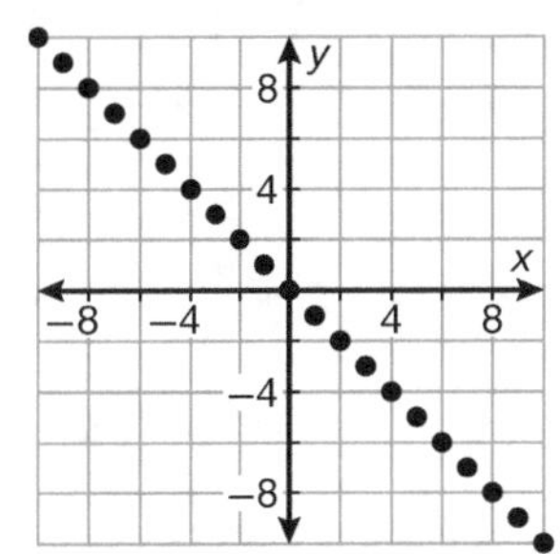

Elements of a Quadratic Function
The **zeros** of a function $f(x)$ are the x-values that make $f(x) = 0$.
The **roots of an equation** are the solutions to the equation.

Square Root Property
If $x^2 = a$, where $a > 0$, then $x = \sqrt{a}$ or $x = -\sqrt{a}$. In general, if $x^2 = a$, then $x = \pm\sqrt{a}$ for any $a > 0$.

Completing the Square
Given a quadratic of the form $x^2 + bx$, add to it the square of half the coefficient of x, $\left(\frac{b}{2}\right)^2$, to create a perfect square trinomial. $x^2 + bx + \left(\frac{b}{2}\right)^2 = \left(x + \frac{b}{2}\right)^2$

Linear/Quadratic Functions

Complex Numbers
A complex number is a number that can be written in the form $a + bi$, where a and b are real numbers. In a complex number, a is called the **real part** and bi is called the **imaginary part.** If $b = 0$, then the imaginary part is 0 and the number is a real number. If $a = 0$ and $b \neq 0$, then the real part is 0 and the number is an imaginary number.

Complex	Real	Imaginary
$2 + 3i$	$2 + 0i = 2$	$0 + 3i = 3i$

Add or Subtract Complex Numbers
$(a + bi) + (c + di) = (a + c) + (b + d)i$ $(a + bi) - (c + di) = (a - c) + (b - d)i$

Absolute Value of a Complex Number

$$|a + bi| = \sqrt{a^2 + b^2}$$

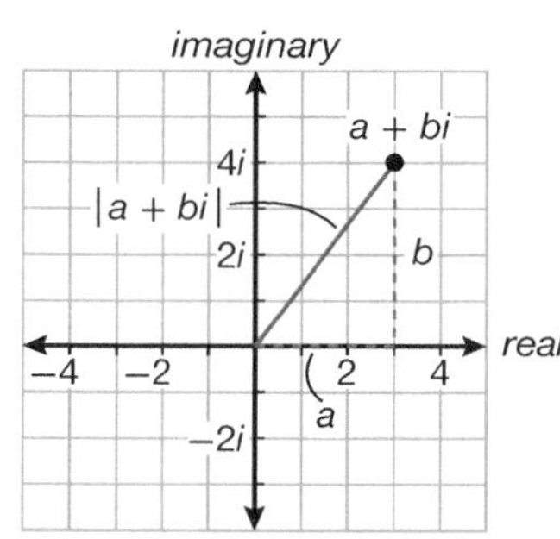

Analyzing the Discriminant		
For $ax^2 + bx + c = 0$, $(a \neq 0)$ and related function $y = ax^2 + bx + c$		
$b^2 - 4ac > 0$	$b^2 - 4ac = 0$	$b^2 - 4ac < 0$
Equation: 2 real roots Function: 2 x-intercepts	Equation: 1 real root with multiplicity of 2 Function: 1 x-intercept	Equation: 0 real roots, 2 complex roots Function: 0 x-intercepts
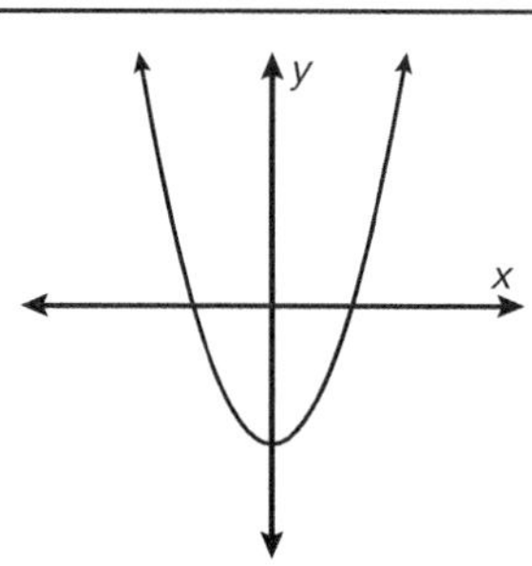	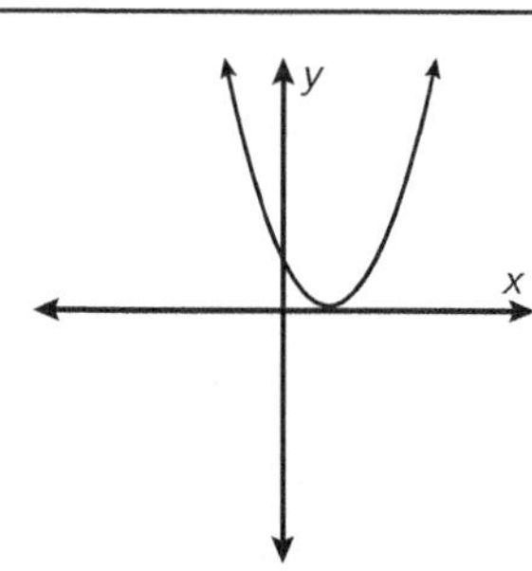	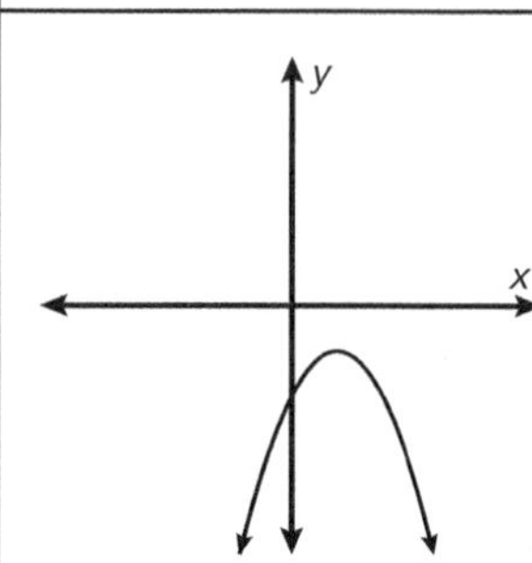

Polynomials and Polynomial Functions

Polynomials
A one-variable polynomial is in **standard form** when all like terms have been combined and its terms are in descending order by degree.
$-x^4 + x^3 - 3x^1 + 2x^0$ ← 4, 3, 1, 0 are in descending order.
A polynomial function is a function of the form
$f(x) = a_n x^n + a_{n-1}x^{n-1} + \ldots + a_1 x + a_0,$
where n is a nonnegative integer and the coefficients $a_n, \ldots, a_0$ are real numbers. The leading coefficient is a_n, the constant term is a_0, and the degree is n.

Difference of Two Squares
$a^2 - b^2 = (a + b)(a - b)$

Sum and Difference of Cubes
Sum of Two Cubes: $a^3 + b^3 = (a + b)(a^2 - ab + b^2)$
Difference of Two Cubes: $a^3 - b^3 = (a - b)(a^2 + ab + b^2)$

Multiplicity of Roots
The multiplicity of a root r of a polynomial equation is the number of times $x - r$ is a factor of the polynomial.

Synthetic Division

To divide polynomial $f(x)$ by $x - k$, begin by writing k and the coefficients of $f(x)$ on the first line.

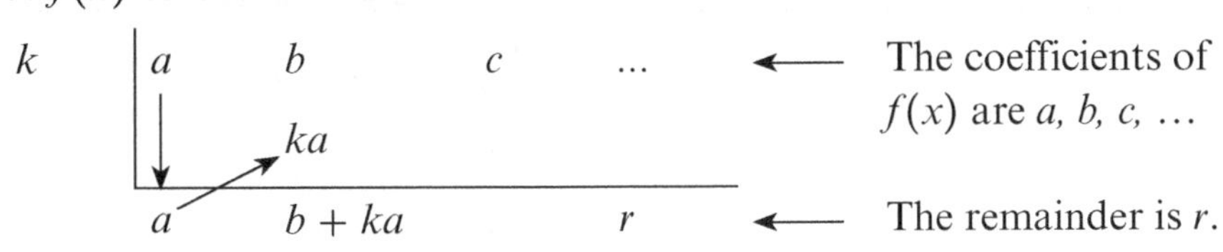

Bring down a; this is the first coefficient of the quotient.

Multiply a by k. Write the result, ka, under b.

Add b and ka. The result, $b + ka$, is the second quotient coefficient.

Continue the pattern. Multiply each new quotient coefficient by k and add the result to the next coefficient of $f(x)$. The result of the last addition is the remainder r.

Polynomials and Polynomial Functions

Name	Theorem	Page
Factor Theorem	For polynomial $P(x)$, $(x - a)$ is a factor of $P(x)$ if and only if $P(a) = 0$.	436
The Rational Root Theorem	If a polynomial $P(x)$ has integer coefficients, then every rational root of $P(x) = 0$ can be written in the form $\frac{p}{q}$, where p is a factor of the constant term and q is a factor of the leading coefficient of $P(x)$.	470
The Irrational Root Theorem	If a polynomial $P(x)$ has rational coefficients, and $a + b\sqrt{c}$ is a root of $P(x) = 0$, where a and b are rational and $\sqrt{c}$ is irrational, then $a - b\sqrt{c}$ is also a root of $P(x) = 0$.	470
Remainder Theorem	The Remainder Theorem states: If polynomial function $P(x)$ is divided by $x - a$, then the remainder r is $P(a)$.	665
The Fundamental Theorem of Algebra	The Fundamental Theorem of Algebra states that every polynomial function of degree $n \geq 1$ has at least one zero in the set of complex numbers. A corollary of the theorem is that, including multiplicities, a polynomial function of degree $n \geq 1$ has exactly n zeros.	738

Rational and Radical Functions

Rational Number	Rational Expression
$\frac{a}{b}$, for integers a and b, $b \neq 0$	$\frac{f(x)}{g(x)}$, for polynomials $f(x)$ and $g(x)$, $g(x) \neq 0$, $g(x)$ of degree ≥ 1

Rational Exponent Property	Properties of *n*th Roots
For m and n integers and $n \neq 0$: $a^{\frac{1}{n}} = \sqrt[n]{a}$ $a^{\frac{m}{n}} = (\sqrt[n]{a})^m = \sqrt[n]{a^m}$	For $a > 0$ and $b > 0$, **Product Property:** $\sqrt[n]{ab} = \sqrt[n]{a} \cdot \sqrt[n]{b}$ **Quotient Property:** $\sqrt[n]{\frac{a}{b}} = \frac{\sqrt[n]{a}}{\sqrt[n]{b}}$

Exponential and Logarithmic Functions

Logarithms
A **logarithm** is the exponent that is applied to a specific base to obtain a given value. Every exponential equation has a logarithmic form and vice versa.
Exponential Equation $\quad$ **Logarithmic Equation**
$\boldsymbol{b^x = a} \quad \boldsymbol{\log_b a = x}$
$b > 0, b \neq 1$

Change of Base Formula
For a > 0 and a $\neq 1$ and any base b such that $b > 0$, and $b \neq 1$, $\log_b x = \frac{\log_a x}{\log_a b}$.

Properties of Logarithms	
Inverse Properties	$b^{\log_b x} = x$ and $\log_b b^x = x$
Product Property	For any positive numbers m, n, and b ($b \neq 1$), $\log_b mn = \log_b m + \log_b n$.
Quotient Property	For any positive numbers m, n, and b ($b \neq 1$), $\log_b \frac{m}{n} = \log_b m - \log_b n$.
Power Property	For any real number p and positive numbers a and b ($b \neq 1$), $\log_b a^p = p\log_b a$.

Properties of Natural Logarithms	
Inverse Properties	$e^{\ln x} = x$ and $\ln e^x = x$, where $x > 0$
Product Property	$\ln ab = \ln a + \ln b$ for any positive numbers a and b.
Quotient Property	$\ln \frac{a}{b} = \ln a - \ln b$ for any positive numbers a and b.
Power Property	$\ln a^p = p \ln a$ for any positive number a and real number p.

Natural Base Functions
$N(t) = N_0 e^{kt}$ is a natural base exponential growth function and $N(t) = N_0 e^{-kt}$ is a natural base exponential decay function, where $N_0 = N(0)$ is the original amount ($t = 0$) and $k > 0$ is a constant.

Linear Systems/Matrices

Parametric Equations	
When two variables are expressed in terms of a third variable, the equations used are called parametric equations.	$x(t) = t + 1$ $y(t) = -2t$

Classifying Systems of Equations		
Types of Lines	**Solution**	**Classification**
Intersecting	Exactly one solution	Consistent and Independent
Coinciding (on top of each other)	Infinite number of solutions	Consistent and Dependent
Parallel	No solutions	Inconsistent

Matrix Addition

To add two matrices, A and B, of the same dimensions, add each element in the first matrix to the element that is in the same location in the second matrix.

$$\begin{bmatrix} a_{11} & a_{12} \\ a_{21} & a_{22} \end{bmatrix} + \begin{bmatrix} b_{11} & b_{12} \\ b_{21} & b_{22} \end{bmatrix} = \begin{bmatrix} a_{11} + b_{11} & a_{12} + b_{12} \\ a_{21} + b_{21} & a_{22} + b_{22} \end{bmatrix}$$

Matrix Subtraction

To subtract two matrices of the same dimensions, $A - B$, take the opposite, or additive inverse, of B and add it to A.

$$\begin{bmatrix} a_{11} & a_{12} \\ a_{21} & a_{22} \end{bmatrix} - \begin{bmatrix} b_{11} & b_{12} \\ b_{21} & b_{22} \end{bmatrix} = \begin{bmatrix} a_{11} + (-b_{11}) & a_{12} + (-b_{12}) \\ a_{21} + (-b_{21}) & a_{22} + (-b_{22}) \end{bmatrix}$$

Matrix Multiplication

Any element in a particular row and column of the product matrix is the sum of the product of the corresponding elements in the corresponding row and column of the matrices being multiplied.

$$\underset{A}{\begin{bmatrix} a & b \\ c & d \end{bmatrix}} \cdot \underset{B}{\begin{bmatrix} e & f \\ g & h \end{bmatrix}} = \underset{AB}{\begin{bmatrix} ae + bg & af + bh \\ ce + dg & cf + dh \end{bmatrix}}$$

Linear Systems/Matrices

Scalar Multiplication
To multiply matrix A by scalar n, multiply every element of A by n.
$n\begin{bmatrix} a_{11} & a_{12} \\ a_{21} & a_{22} \end{bmatrix} = \begin{bmatrix} n \cdot a_{11} & n \cdot a_{12} \\ n \cdot a_{21} & n \cdot a_{22} \end{bmatrix}$

Matrix Multiplicative Identity
The product of any matrix A and the multiplicative identity matrix I is matrix A.
$AI = IA = A$

Matrix Determinant
For a square 2×2 matrix such as $\begin{bmatrix} a & b \\ c & d \end{bmatrix}$, the determinant equals $ad - cb$.

Cramer's Rule
The solutions of the linear system $\begin{matrix} ax + by = e \\ cx + dy = f \end{matrix}$ are
$x = \dfrac{\begin{vmatrix} e & b \\ f & d \end{vmatrix}}{D}$ and $y = \dfrac{\begin{vmatrix} a & e \\ c & f \end{vmatrix}}{D}$, where D is the determinant of the coefficient matrix.

Classifying Systems by Their Solutions	
If both x and y have the form $\frac{\not{0}}{\not{0}}$, …	then the system has exactly one solution.
If both x and y have the form $\frac{\not{0}}{0}$, …	then the system has no solution.
If either x or y has the form $\frac{0}{0}$, …	then the system has an infinite number of solution.

Inverse of a 2 × 2 Matrix
If $A = \begin{bmatrix} a & b \\ c & d \end{bmatrix}$ and $ad - cb \neq 0$, then the inverse of A is:
$A^{-1} = \frac{1}{\lvert A \rvert}\begin{bmatrix} d & -b \\ -c & a \end{bmatrix} = \frac{1}{ad - cb}\begin{bmatrix} d & -b \\ -c & a \end{bmatrix}.$

Using an Inverse to Solve a Matrix Equation		
If matrix A has an inverse and the matrix equation $AX = B$ has a solution, then the solution is $X = A^{-1}B$.	$AX = B$	
	$A^{-1}AX = A^{-1}B$	Multiply both sides by A^{-1}.
	$IX = A^{-1}B$	$A^{-1}A = I$ by definition of inverse.
	$X = A^{-1}B$	$IX = X$ by definition of identity.

Linear Systems/Matrices

Vector Addition	Vector Subtraction
$\begin{bmatrix} x_1 \\ y_1 \end{bmatrix} + \begin{bmatrix} x_2 \\ y_2 \end{bmatrix} = \begin{bmatrix} x_1 + x_2 \\ y_1 + y_2 \end{bmatrix}$	$\begin{bmatrix} x_1 \\ y_1 \end{bmatrix} - \begin{bmatrix} x_2 \\ y_2 \end{bmatrix} = \begin{bmatrix} x_1 - x_2 \\ y_1 - y_2 \end{bmatrix}$
$(a + bi) + (c + di) = (a + c) + (b + d)i$	$(a + bi) - (c + di) = (a - c) + (b - d)i$

Vector Addition

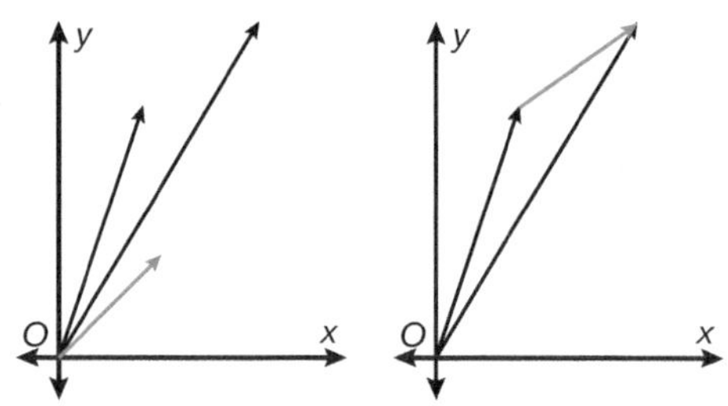

Vector Subtraction

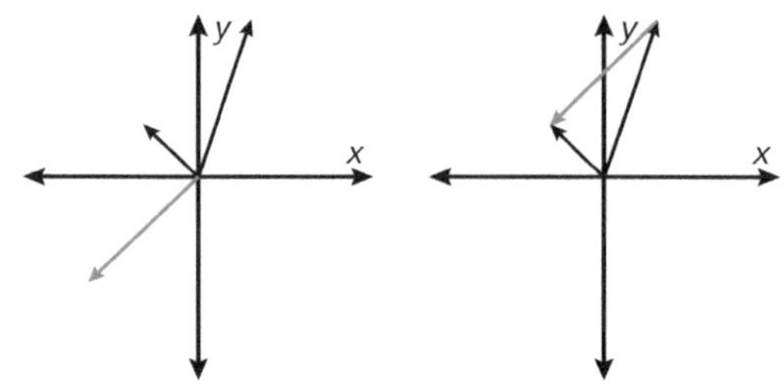

Dot Product
$A \cdot B = \lvert A \rvert \lvert B \rvert \cos \theta$

Conic Sections

Standard Forms for Conic Sections with Center (h, k)		
Circle	$(x - h)^2 + (y - k)^2 = r^2$	
	Horizontal Axis	**Vertical Axis**
Ellipse	$\frac{(x-h)^2}{a^2} + \frac{(y-k)^2}{b^2} = 1; a > b$	$\frac{(x-h)^2}{b^2} + \frac{(y-k)^2}{a^2} = 1; a > b$
Hyperbola	$\frac{(x-h)^2}{a^2} - \frac{(y-k)^2}{b^2} = 1$	$\frac{(y-k)^2}{a^2} - \frac{(x-h)^2}{b^2} = 1$
Parabola	$x - h = \frac{1}{\pm 4p}(y - k)^2$	$y - k = \frac{1}{\pm 4p}(x - h)^2$

Standard Form of the Equation of an Ellipse: Center at (0, 0)	
Major Axis Horizontal	**Major Axis Vertical**
$\frac{x^2}{a^2} + \frac{y^2}{b^2} = 1$	$\frac{y^2}{a^2} + \frac{x^2}{b^2} = 1$
Vertices: $(a, 0), (-a, 0)$	Vertices: $(0, a), (0, -a)$
Foci: $(c, 0), (-c, 0)$	Foci: $(0\ c\ ), (0, -c)$
Co-vertices: $(0, b), (0, -b)$	Co-vertices: $(b, 0), (-b, 0)$

Trigonometry

Definition of Trigonometric Functions		
For a point $Q(x, y)$ on the terminal side of θ in standard position and $r = \sqrt{x^2 + y^2}$,		
$\sin\theta = \frac{y}{r}$	$\cos\theta = \frac{x}{r}$	$\tan\theta = \frac{y}{x}, x \neq 0$

Converting Angle Measures	
Degrees to Radians	**Radians to Degrees**
Multiply the number of degrees by $\left(\frac{\pi \text{ radians}}{180°}\right)$.	Multiply the number of radians by $\left(\frac{180°}{\pi \text{ radians}}\right)$.

The Unit Circle

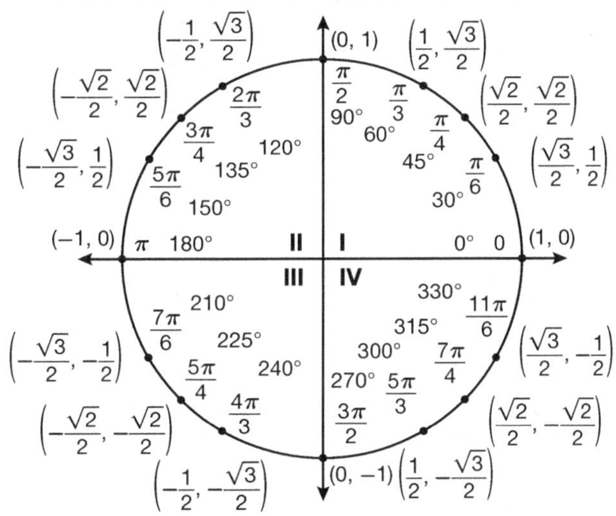

Arc Length Formula

For a circle of radius r, the **arc length** s intercepted by a central angle θ (measured in radians) is given by the following formula.

$$s = r\theta$$

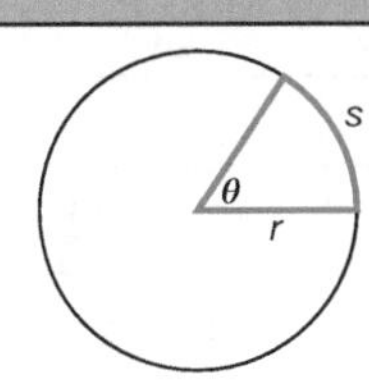

Inverse Trigonometric Functions

Words	Symbol	Domain	Range
The **inverse sine function** is $\text{Sin}^{-1}a = \theta$, where $\text{Sin}\,\theta = a$.	$\text{Sin}^{-1}a$	$\{a \mid -1 \leq a \leq 1\}$	$\left\{\theta \mid -\frac{\pi}{2} \leq \theta \leq \frac{\pi}{2}\right\}$ $\{\theta \mid -90° \leq \theta \leq 90°\}$
The **inverse cosine function** is $\text{Cos}^{-1}a = \theta$, where $\text{Cos}\,\theta = a$.	$\text{Cos}^{-1}a$	$\{a \mid -1 \leq a \leq 1\}$	$\{\theta \mid 0 \leq \theta \leq \pi\}$ $\{\theta \mid 0° \leq \theta \leq 180°\}$
The **inverse tangent function** is $\text{Tan}^{-1}a = \theta$, where $\text{Tan}\,\theta = a$.	$\text{Tan}^{-1}a$	$\{a \mid -\infty < a < \infty\}$	$\left\{\theta \mid -\frac{\pi}{2} < \theta < \frac{\pi}{2}\right\}$ $\{\theta \mid -90° < \theta < 90°\}$

ALGEBRA 2

Trigonometry

Area of a Triangle

Area $= \frac{1}{2}bc \sin A$

Area $= \frac{1}{2}ac \sin B$

Area $= \frac{1}{2}ab \sin C$

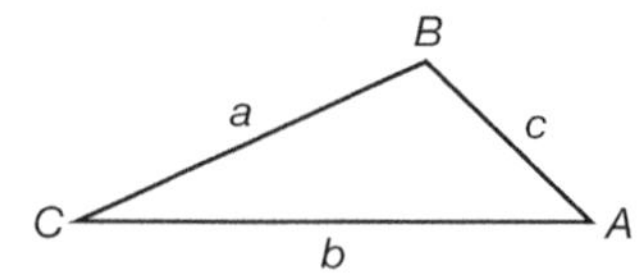

Heron's Formula

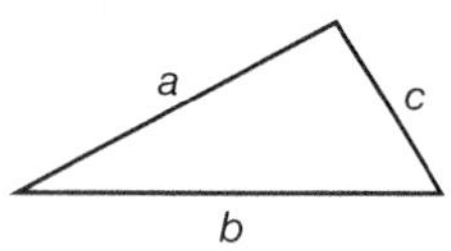

$A = \sqrt{s(s-a)(s-b)(s-c)}$, where

$s = \dfrac{1}{2}(a + b + c)$.

Possible Triangles Given SSA

Given a, c, and $m\angle A$ in $\triangle ABC$,
If $h < a < c$, then there are two possible triangles where:

- $h = c \sin A$
- The sum of the measures of $\angle C$ in each triangle is 180°.

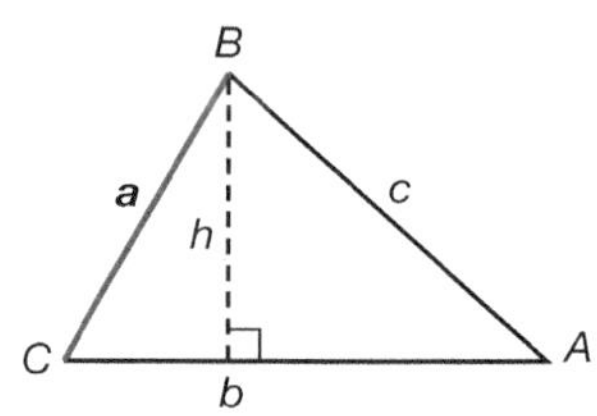

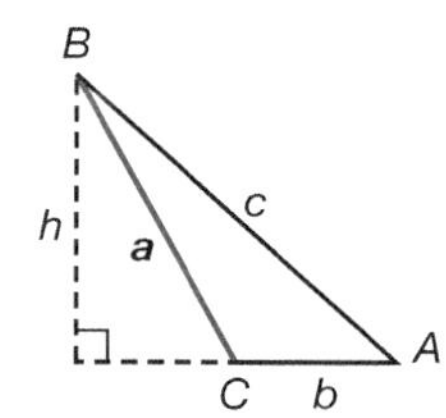

Properties of Sine and Cosine Graphs

For the graphs of $y = a \sin bx$ or $y = a \cos bx$ where x is in radians and $a \neq 0$

- the amplitude is $|a|$.
- the number of cycles in the interval from 0 to 2π is b.
- the period is $\frac{2\pi}{b}$.

Sine and Cosine Functions in Standard Form

$y = a \sin b(x - h) + k$ $\qquad$ $y = a \cos b(x - h) + k$

The measure of angle x is in radians. $|a|$ = amplitude, the vertical stretch or shrink of the graph of the function, $\frac{2\pi}{b}$ = period, where $b > 0$, h = horizontal or phase shift, and k = vertical shift.

Properties of Tangent Functions

If $y = a \tan bx$, with $b > 0$

- $\frac{\pi}{b}$ is the period of the function
- One cycle occurs in the interval from $-\frac{\pi}{2b}$ to $\frac{\pi}{2b}$
- Vertical asymptotes occur at each end of the cycle

Trigonometry

Converting Coordinates	
Polar to Cartesian $x = r\cos\theta$ $y = r\sin\theta$	**Cartesian to Polar** $\tan\theta = \frac{y}{x}$ $r^2 = x^2 + y^2$

Using a Rotation Matrix
Let $P(x, y)$ be any point in a plane. Let $P'(x', y')$ be the image of P after a rotation of θ degrees counterclockwise about the origin. Then $\begin{bmatrix} \cos\theta & -\sin\theta \\ \sin\theta & \cos\theta \end{bmatrix}\begin{bmatrix} x \\ y \end{bmatrix} = \begin{bmatrix} x' \\ y' \end{bmatrix}$.

Double-Angle Identities		
$\sin 2\theta = 2\sin\theta\cos\theta$	$\cos 2\theta = \cos^2\theta - \sin^2\theta$ $\cos 2\theta = 2\cos^2\theta - 1$ $\cos 2\theta = 1 - 2\sin^2\theta$	$\tan 2\theta = \frac{2\tan\theta}{1 - \tan^2\theta}$

Half-Angle Identities
$\sin\frac{\theta}{2} = \pm\sqrt{\frac{1 - \cos\theta}{2}}$ $\quad\cos\frac{\theta}{2} = \pm\sqrt{\frac{1 + \cos\theta}{2}}$ $\quad\tan\frac{\theta}{2} = \pm\sqrt{\frac{1 - \cos\theta}{1 + \cos\theta}}$
Choose + or − depending on the location of $\frac{\theta}{2}$.

Sum and Difference Identities	
Sum Identities	**Difference Identities**
$\sin(A + B) = \sin A\cos B + \cos A\sin B$	$\sin(A - B) = \sin A\cos B - \cos A\sin B$
$\cos(A + B) = \cos A\cos B - \sin A\sin B$	$\cos(A - B) = \cos A\cos B + \sin A\sin B$
$\tan(A + B) = \frac{\tan A + \tan B}{1 - \tan A\tan B}$	$\tan(A - B) = \frac{\tan A - \tan B}{1 + \tan A\tan B}$

Probability and Statistics

Measures of Dispersion
The **range of a data set** is the difference between the largest and smallest data values.
The **variance** of a data set is the average of the squared differences from the mean.
The **standard deviation** measures, on average, how far away from the mean the data values are. The standard deviation σ, which is the Greek letter sigma, is the square root of the variance and is calculated using the following formula for a data set with n terms, $x_1, x_2, \ldots, x_n$: $$\sigma = \sqrt{\frac{(x_1 - \overline{x})^2 + (x_2 - \overline{x})^2 + \ldots (x_n - \overline{x})^2}{n}}$$
An **outlier** is an item in a data set that is much larger or much smaller than the other items in the set. The presence of an outlier in a set of data can have a misleading effect on the measures of central tendency and dispersion.

Standard Deviations and the Normal Bell Curve

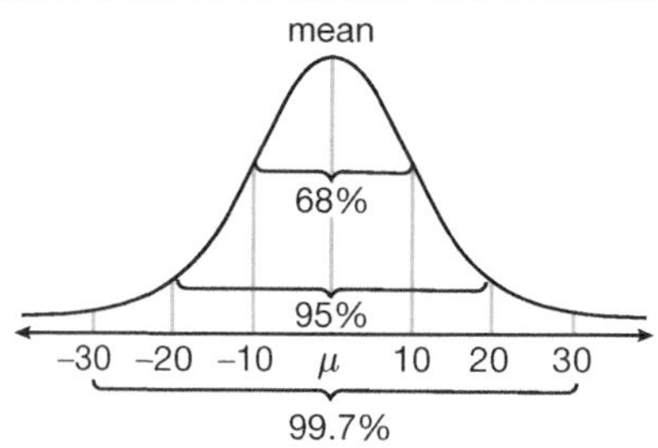

z-score
Given that x is a data value of a normally distributed set of data, the $$z\text{-score} = \frac{x - \text{mean}}{\text{standard deviation}}.$$

Addition Counting Principle
Suppose a trial can result in any of n_1 outcomes from one category, any of n_2 outcomes from another category, and so on. If there are k different categories of outcomes, then the total number of outcomes that can result is $n_1 + n_2 + \ldots + n_k$.

Fundamental Counting Principle
Suppose k items are to be chosen. If there are n_1 ways to choose the first item, n_2 ways to choose the second item, and so on, then there are $n_1 \cdot n_2 \cdot \ldots \cdot n_k$ ways to choose all k items.

Probability and Statistics

n Factorial
The factorial of n is denoted as $n!$ $n! = n(n-1)(n-2)(n-3)\ldots 1$ Zero factorial is defined to be 1. $0! = 1$.

Permutations
The permutation of n objects taken r at a time is: $P(n, r) = \frac{n!}{(n-r)!}$

Combinations
The combination of n objects taken r at a time is: $C(n, r) = \frac{n!}{r!(n-r)!}$

Binomial Theorem
If n is a nonnegative integer, then $(a+b)^n = ({}_nC_0)a^nb^0 + ({}_nC_1)a^{n-1}b^1 + ({}_nC_2)a^{n-2}b^2 + \ldots + ({}_nC_{n-1})a^1b^{n-1} + ({}_nC_n)a^0b^n$ $= \sum_{r=0}^{n}({}_nC_r)a^{n-r}b^r$ where ${}_nC_r = \frac{n!}{r!(n-r)!}$

Binomial Probability
If p is the probability of success and q is the probability of failure in one trial of a binomial experiment, then the **binomial probability** of exactly n successes in m trials is given by ${}_mC_np^nq^{m-n}$.

ALGEBRA 2

Sequences, Series, and Logic

Summation Notation
For the series $\sum_{k=1}^{n} a_k = a_1 + a_2 + a_3 + \ldots + a_n$, the integer k is called the index, 1 is the lower limit of summation, and n is the upper limit of summation.

Sum of a Finite Arithmetic Series
The sum of the first n terms of an arithmetic series, S_n, is $\frac{n}{2}(a_1 + a_n)$.

Sum of a Finite Geometric Series
The sum of the first n terms of a geometric series, S_n, is $a_1\left(\frac{1 - r^n}{1 - r}\right)$.

Sum of an Infinite Geometric Series
The sum of an infinite geometric series, S, is $\frac{a_1}{1 - r}$, where r is the common ratio and $0 < \lvert r \rvert < 1$.